Praise for *The EQ Prescription*

"Dr. Lebowitz brilliantly adds to the compelling discussion as to why patients come second. A must-read for everyone in health care who will absolutely benefit greatly by adhering to the valuable prescription to put themselves first."

—Paul Spiegelman, best-selling author of
Patients Come Second; co-founder, Kintsugi Village;
co-founder Small Giants Community; founder,
BerylHealth and the Beryl Institute

"This book is a master class for all health-care professionals. The real-life experiences and takeaways for clinicians, nurses, and students capture the essence of health care today and its future. As a nurse for many years, I saw myself in many of the examples and will be sure I stay in the Zone. This book challenges you to reflect on becoming more self-aware, recognizing emotions in others so you can build stronger relationships."

—Lynne Shopiro, RN, chief
nursing officer, Crouse Hospital

"*The EQ Prescription* is a timely and essential guide for anyone navigating the emotional complexities of a career in health care. Dr. Lebowitz offers a practical and empowering framework to help clinicians, educators, and students stay grounded, resilient, and effective even amid the stressors that define our profession. Through the lens of the EQ Zone, he reframes wellness as not just a personal goal but a clinical imperative. This book will change how health-care professionals think about self-management and emotional performance in the workplace, and it couldn't come at a better time."

—Michael Roscoe, PhD, PA-C, associate clinical professor of family medicine; director of simulation, Indiana University School of Medicine—Evansville; long-standing PA program director and national PA education leader

"*The EQ Prescription* is a powerful guide for staying grounded in the demanding world of health care. Dr. Lebowitz distills complex emotional intelligence concepts into practical tools that help clinicians, nurses, and students thrive—improving team dynamics and patient care."

—Seth Kronenberg, MD, president and CEO, Crouse Health

"It was a treat to read *The EQ Prescription*. I loved the premise of the EQ Zone. The concept is easy to grasp, and best of all, the 'prescription' can be used immediately. The writing is excellent, very readable, and gets right to the point, a real bonus for clinicians, nurses, and students in health care who may have limited time. In writing this book, Dr. Lebowitz shares his genuine passion and deep caring for those who deliver health care and describes why it is so important and beneficial to put yourself first and that patients come second."

—**Britt Berrett,** PhD, FACHE, managing
director and teaching professor, BYU
Marriott School of Business; best-selling
author of *Patients Come Second*

The EQ Prescription

Put Yourself First to Thrive in Health Care

Mickey Lebowitz, MD

RIVER GROVE
BOOKS

This publication is designed to provide accurate and authoritative information in regard to the subject matter covered. It is sold with the understanding that the publisher and author are not engaged in rendering legal, accounting, or other professional services. Nothing herein shall create an attorney-client relationship, and nothing herein shall constitute legal advice or a solicitation to offer legal advice. If legal advice or other expert assistance is required, the services of a competent professional should be sought.

Published by River Grove Books
Austin, TX
www.rivergrovebooks.com

Distributed by River Grove Books

Design and composition by Greenleaf Book Group
Cover design by Greenleaf Book Group
Cover images used under license from ©Adobestock.com

Publisher's Cataloging-in-Publication data is available.

Print ISBN: 978-1-966629-53-5

eBook ISBN: 978-1-966629-54-2

First Edition

*My book is dedicated to my clinician and nurse peers,
my students, and my patients who have taught me so much
over the years while also inspiring and motivating me
to be the best clinician, educator, and person I could possibly be.
I am grateful for how you all enriched my life personally
and professionally and helped me better serve.*

Contents

Foreword

by Joshua Freedman, CEO, Six Seconds

Health care is a field defined by people. From patients to providers to support staff, every aspect of the system depends on human interaction. It's not just technical skill or medical knowledge that makes the work effective; it's the ability to work *with* and *through* people. And that means health care is also defined by emotion.

This emotional layer is both the challenge and the opportunity. Every day in health care, people navigate high-stakes situations filled with vulnerability, urgency, and sometimes grief or frustration. It's no wonder that so many feel overwhelmed, numb, or burned out. For some, the response is to withdraw from these emotional complexities, protecting themselves by disconnecting. But there's a cost to that approach: Empathy erodes, communication suffers, and well-being declines.

Dr. Mickey Lebowitz, also referred to affectionately by so many as Dr. Mickey, offers a better way forward: Don't shut down; *get smarter with feelings*. Rather than avoiding emotions, we can become more skilled at navigating them. That's the essence of emotional intelligence. And in this book, Dr. Mickey shows how to apply that intelligence to one of the most emotionally demanding professions on the planet.

His model, the EQ Zone, is both insightful and practical. It gives health-care professionals a structure for noticing when they're at their best and what bumps them out of that space. It's a tool for recognizing emotional cues, responding with more intention, and staying grounded even in the chaos of modern medicine. It's a way to be more effective and more human.

As someone who's been working in emotional intelligence for nearly three decades, I'm thrilled by how Dr. Mickey makes these concepts come alive. This isn't just theory: It's real-world guidance that works in hospitals, clinics, classrooms, and homes. His voice is relatable, honest, and rooted in lived experience. He's gone through the ringer, so you don't have to. You just have to be someone who's trying to show up, every day, in the middle of a demanding and often thankless system.

At Six Seconds, we define emotional intelligence as being smarter with feelings. We use the abbreviation EQ in parallel to IQ. EQ is a form of intelligence, just like IQ. In fact, all forms of intelligence share the same process:

1. Acquire accurate data.

2. Appraise the data meaningfully.

3. Apply the data to create better outcomes.

You can be intelligent about systems. You can be intelligent about biology. And you can be intelligent about emotion. What Dr. Mickey shows in these pages is that emotional intelligence follows the same structure; it just requires practice.

That's the core of our work at Six Seconds, a nonprofit organization dedicated to supporting people to develop and apply emotional intelligence in practical ways. We work in every country and territory to grow the world's emotional intelligence. We do this in a wide range of organizations, including health care. In addition, we equip professionals with tools and methods for their work—and we bring emotional intelligence to nonprofits and communities to support youth well-being.

At Six Seconds, our model follows three steps:

1. **Know Yourself**—Increase awareness of emotions and reactions. Acquire accurate data.

2. **Choose Yourself**—Build intentionality. Appraise what matters most and how to respond with clarity.

3. **Give Yourself**—Act with empathy and purpose. Apply emotional insight to create stronger relationships and more sustainable impact.

At Six Seconds, our vision is a billion people practicing emotional intelligence. Not just knowing about it, but actively following those three steps to be more aware, more intentional, and more purposeful. With this book, Dr. Mickey is helping make that vision real. He's bringing emotional intelligence to a field that urgently needs it, and doing so in a way that is accessible, compassionate, and powerful.

Health care is a prime arena for that practice. Why? Because it's deeply emotional and highly relational. The stakes are high, the pace is intense, and the people delivering care are often under immense pressure.

That's why this book is so important. It offers a kind of prescription, not for patients, but for those delivering the care. And like the best prescriptions, it's not just about masking symptoms. It's about healing and strengthening from within.

So my invitation to you is this: don't just read this book. *Use it.* Try the practices. Reflect on the stories. Notice your own "zone" and what narrows or expands it. This isn't another thing to add to your to-do list:

It's a way to make that list feel more doable, more human, more in tune with your purpose.

In a time when so many in health care feel overwhelmed, this book is a reminder that we don't have to shut down to survive. We can stay open. We can stay connected. And we can become more skillful in navigating the emotional realities of care. That's what emotional intelligence offers. That's what Dr. Mickey Lebowitz has captured in these pages. And that's what I hope you'll discover, page by page.

Introduction

What really matters for success, character, happiness and lifelong achievements is a definite set of emotional skills—your EQ—not just purely cognitive abilities that are measured by conventional IQ tests.

—DANIEL GOLEMAN

If you work in health care, your free time is limited and valuable. So let me cut to the chase and tell you exactly what's in this book for you: a structure and strategy called the Emotional Intelligence Zone, or EQ Zone, which can be used in real time, especially when your daily stress levels are very high. And in the American health-care system, they are always high.

This book is for all types of clinicians, nurses, and students in health-care education programs in every discipline, who all face similar stresses, strains, pressures, and high stakes. It is intended for medical professionals, and those up and coming, who would like to take better care of themselves and, consequently, their current and future patients by more effectively managing themselves through the intense ups and downs, highs and lows, and the inevitable, inescapable pain points that are endemic to our field.

Using the EQ Zone will help everyone associated with health care to maintain wellness and be (even more) successful delivering the care that they would like to deliver, and that patients would like to receive. To give your best, you have to be your best, and to be your best, you have to be emotionally *and* physically well. *The Emotional Intelligence Zone helps you do both.*[1]

In short, this book is about how to be smarter with your emotions so as to manage the long list of situations and pain points that we in health care have little, if any, control over. As described in the 2024 Medscape Physician Burnout and Depression Report, the list includes required bureaucratic tasks such as charting and paperwork; lack of respect from administration, employers, colleagues, staff, and patients; general lack of control and autonomy; insufficient compensation; EMR (electronic medical record) challenges; and government regulations.[2]

Other pain points might include patients not being adherent or diligent with their treatment plan or missing scheduled appointments; staff not showing up to work, leaving everyone shorthanded; and some unscheduled something that seemingly always interrupts and negatively impacts your day, making a hard day caring for your patients harder.

These difficulties lead clinicians, nurses, and health-care students to experience high levels of dissatisfaction, burnout, and depression; cutting back to fewer workdays; or prematurely exiting their practices.[3] Despite the multitude of potentially sensible strategies described in the Medscape 2024 report to manage these challenges (exercise, talking with family and friends, sleeping, spending time alone, playing or listening to music, meditating, using prescription drugs), and even the less sensible, potentially harmful strategies (eating junk food and binge eating, drinking alcohol, smoking or using nicotine products),[4] it is clear that using these strategies to manage health care's pain points hasn't meaningfully, statistically, moved the needle.

This failure has led to the discouraging and disheartening comments highlighted in the Medscape 2024 report such as the following: "I have lost my desire to help and innovate," "I arrive at work every day trying to have a good outlook, but it only lasts fifteen seconds," "I count down the hours until I can leave, and I am unhappy talking to people," and "Work has become something I totally dread. There is too much pressure to do too much, with so little staff and resources. All with the possibility of a lawsuit over your head."[5]

According to Software Advice's 2023 Nursing Pain Point Survey conducted in December 2022, nurses' top three pain points were caring for too many patients in a day (61 percent), hours spent on administrative tasks (60 percent), and increased workload due to co-workers leaving (59 percent).[6] Nurses are also concerned with unsafe working conditions that lead to musculoskeletal and sharp injuries and workplace violence.[7]

Students in health-care education programs are not immune to pain points either. They often have more to do and learn than time allows, leaving little time for socializing, or self-care; they are required to take and pass endless exams and assessments; their class times and lengths are out of their control; they are periodically put on the spot, tested and judged by professors and preceptors on how they answer medical knowledge questions, present their cases, and manage their patients; and on occasion, they are harassed sexually and otherwise.

This book will not make you more technically competent or make these pain points go away. The latter would be in the purview of the people who organize, oversee, and administer health care. Rather, it will help you to be more emotionally competent to manage these pain points better. People tend to do better work when they feel better about the work they are doing. I'm optimistic that learning about, and using, the EQ

Zone will allow you to feel and work (even) better to your benefit and the benefit of your patients. Yogi Berra, the Hall of Fame baseball player and pseudo philosopher, may have emphasized and summarized the value of emotional competence and performance best when he said, "Baseball is ninety percent mental. The other half is physical."[8]

As a bonus, the skills this book will offer you don't just disappear when you leave the hospital, office, clinic, skilled nursing facility, home care, or school. They are usable and transferable to all areas of your personal life, enriching your decision-making abilities to achieve better results; influencing others to produce positive impact; developing and maintaining relationships with people in your community and your network; helping you to increase your physical and emotional health and balance of life; and finally enabling you to achieve and feel more satisfied with your life.

You may curiously ask, "Who is Mickey Lebowitz and what education and experiences give him credibility to enlighten me on the EQ Zone?" I welcome your curiosity. To answer, I'd like to share with you a bit about my journey to the EQ Zone, which started even before EQ and the Zone were terms.

My Journey to the EQ Zone

Growing up in the Canarsie section of Brooklyn, New York, in the 1960s, I experienced the power of emotional intelligence informally, and way before the term "emotional intelligence" was coined in 1990 by Peter Salovey and John Mayer, and later popularized by Daniel Goleman in his 1995 book *Emotional Intelligence*. As a young boy, I lived on a block with a lot of kids my age. We were always in the street, playing sports like punchball, sponge ball, football, basketball, and more. Invariably, my friends and I would get into a little kerfuffle arguing about balls and strikes, or whether there was a traveling violation or a foul or if the thrown football pass was caught in bounds or not. These would lead to arguments and occasional fisticuffs.

Afterward my mom, who was innately emotionally aware and intelligent, able to cannily see things from others' points of view, would talk with me about the emotional elements in the situation. She usually began by asking how I felt. "Mickey, what are you feeling?" She would make me name it. Then, "Where is that feeling coming from?"—pushing and helping me to hone my emotional literacy skills. Other emotionally oriented questions shortly followed, such as "How do you think the other kid might be feeling?" and "How could you have managed the situation differently?" She also asked me to think about the other kid, about what hard family times they were going through just then. Certainly, this was my first introduction to empathy. These early fundamental and foundational lessons from my mom started me on my journey to self- and social awareness, self- and relationship management, and self-direction, which benefited me in many ways in my personal and professional life.

Despite my mom's tutelage and guidance, and without any formal EQ training—not even knowing that formal training existed—I basically used wit and instinct to navigate my emotions. However, as time elapsed and challenging situations continued to find me, like bees to honey, I realized I wanted something more formal and definable, like a structure with a strategy to fall back on. I wasn't satisfied that I was optimally handling emotionally charged situations wherever they might originate, professionally or personally. Then I heard about emotional intelligence from a friend who also informed me that EQ is a competency that anyone can improve upon with effort and desire. I was intrigued and hoped that studying and applying emotional intelligence could help me develop the skills that I longed for, that would help me be better, especially during the most stressful times. And it did, exceeding all my expectations.

My education in emotional intelligence began in 2018 with a non-profit multinational company called Six Seconds.⁹ With Six Seconds' guidance and hours upon hours of experiential learning, I earned multiple certifications in the field of emotional intelligence, becoming an EQ practitioner, assessor, facilitator, and certified coach with the International Coaching Federation. I've coached countless clinicians, nurses, physician assistant students, and non-clinicians while also giving numerous EQ Zone presentations and workshops locally and nationally. I've learned much about these professionals (and myself) through listening to their stories and witnessing their growth during those precious "aha" lightbulb moments.

Another reason why I am sharing this knowledge and insight with you is because I made a promise to myself, my profession, and my teammates of clinicians, nurses, and patients that when I left my private endocrine practice in 2007, I would remain committed, dedicated, and loyal, continuing to play for and with them albeit from a different position on the field. After seventeen years of clinical practice, admittedly, I was beaten down, broken up, and burnt out. I wrote the book *Losing My Patience: Why I Quit the Medical Game*, which highlighted, using many sports metaphors, the health-care system's "team" of payers, politicians, pharmaceutical companies, and plaintiffs and their dominant control over my team then and still now.¹⁰

At first, I played for my team locally as the senior medical quality director at my hospital, putting systems in place to make our patients' care safer while also streamlining our clinicians' and nurses' processes and adding efficiency to their workdays (trying to take the pebble out of their shoe). While successful, it wasn't enough. I still witnessed how the health-care system took its toll on the entire staff in so many ways: the mandate to institute then learn how to use electronic medical records with all its limitations and frustrations (even when it is functioning normally) necessitating changes in clinician, nurse, and staff workflow that led to a few of our senior clinicians calling it quits; or seeing patients being readmitted because they couldn't afford the high prices of medications that pharma puts on them; or the "game" of using the correct medical lingo/terminology in our medical records to get maximally paid from the payers for the care of our patients even if it didn't affect the good care that we were already giving our patients; or the moral injury of playing defensive medicine, ordering additional potentially unnecessary tests to cover ourselves, "just in case," and offset the risk of malpractice.

Even more upsetting was that the clinicians, nurses, and staff at our hospital were some of the kindest, most compassionate, smartest, and talented people I have ever met. I was honored to be associated with them. It was heartbreaking to see them in the same way I saw myself as I was leaving private practice. I wanted to do more, and more needed to be done, to help them survive and thrive, so I went looking for more to do to assist my team. That's when I learned about the value and enormous benefits of emotional intelligence (detailed in Chapters 5 and 6). I found my new position on the field to help my team locally and beyond.

What I learned about emotional intelligence in health care was best summarized by an edgy title of a book by Britt Berrett and Paul Spiegelman, *Patients Come Second.*[11] Though on first look this might sound like heresy (don't patients come first?!), they reasoned that for patients to be satisfied with their care, and receive the care they desire, the people who are delivering the care must work in an excellent organizational culture and climate—where they can do their best work—facilitated by leaders dedicated and loyal to their clinicians, nurses, and staff and develop that positive work environment. In essence, their "prescription" for excellent patient care was, ironically, for patients to come second, because the people delivering the care must come first. My book has a similar "prescription" (also with an edgy title), *Put Yourself First*, which takes the theme from *Patients Come Second* to the next level and adds a little twist. In short, for you to thrive in health care, doing your best work, delivering the care that you want to deliver and that your patients want to receive, you *must* put yourself first and be able to manage yourself through health care's pain points. If you are not in your zone and not your very best, it is very hard to give your best and for your patients to receive your best, which, I believe, is the goal of every clinician, nurse, and clinician/nurse-to-be.

Unfortunately, I have seen the unintended harmful consequences when those who are affected by these pain points are not able to manage them and care for themselves first. Those consequences can include friction with co-workers, unprofessional behaviors, poor patient outcomes, malpractice cases, failing classes, burnout, and much more. Admittedly, I have not been immune to being emotionally blind in my career. I have had my share of vulnerable moments reacting to these pain points that narrowed or bumped me out of my zone, which I will share with you via stories throughout this book, that led to unintended consequences, regrets, remorse, and also the desire to improve and be better. Wishing that I knew then what I know now is another reason I am writing this book, to help prevent you from repeating my missteps.

Therefore, I encourage you to read on and benefit from what this book has to offer you. Learn **what** the emotional intelligence zone is (Part I), **why** it matters to you (Part II), and **how** to get better at applying it (Part III). All I ask of you as you read through the book is this: Stay engaged, open-minded, and curious about the concepts while considering all the possibilities and reflecting on ways to bring true value to your professional life and beyond. In the end, the main message in this book comes down to this: What can you and what can't you control? The simple answer is only YOU. By being more in control of yourself first, you will be better able to manage and navigate health care's pain points, leading to your enhanced job satisfaction, reducing your risk of burnout and malpractice, and greater patient satisfaction and outcomes.

How can you be more in control of yourself, in real time, which will help you take better care of yourself and be your best more often? It's using the emotional intelligence zone, an additional method, beyond the sensible, and certainly the less sensible strategies described above in the Medscape 2024 report. The EQ zone offers: (1) developing more self- and social awareness; (2) being more intentional with your decisions, leading toward better self- and relationship management; and (3) enhanced self-direction, truly knowing what you want and want to avoid, all leading to keeping your zone wide for longer, and therefore less likely to get triggered and bumped out of your zone. If you are ready to jump in and go on this amazing journey with me to help you put and take care of yourself first, leading to being your best, giving your best, and the associated benefits to you and your patients, turn the page and let's begin.

WELCOME TO THE EQ ZONE

Chapter 1

What Is "The Zone"?

Watch your thoughts, they become your words;
watch your words, they become your actions;
watch your actions, they become your habits;
watch your habits, they become your character;
watch your character, for it becomes your destiny.

—LAO TZU

A common refrain from athletes who are making all their shots playing basketball, hitting home runs in succession playing baseball, or completing every pass playing football is that they were in their zone. During those exceptional moments, they were at their absolute best and just couldn't miss. The fans, in appreciation and awe, go wild watching them. However, athletes don't stay in that rarefied space indefinitely. They inevitably go back to "being human," making some shots and missing others, hitting home runs and then striking out, and connecting on some passes while not completing others. It's part of the game: some-times you win and sometimes you lose.

Unfortunately, we in health care don't have that luxury. We aren't playing in a game. We need to be in our zones as often as humanly possible, even if there aren't people in the stands cheering us on. When we miss, the stakes and consequences are much higher than missing a shot, striking out, throwing an incomplete pass, or losing a competition. Being in our zone and functioning at our best needs to be our standard, not our exception.

You may appropriately ask, what is the zone, and what does it mean for us in health care to be in the zone?

Elaine Miller-Karas is an internationally known trauma therapist and key developer of the Trauma Resiliency Model and Community Resiliency Model. She, along with Peter Levine, Diane Heller, and Genie Everett, designed a visual to represent the Resilient Zone, also referred to as "The Zone" (see Figure 1.1).[1]

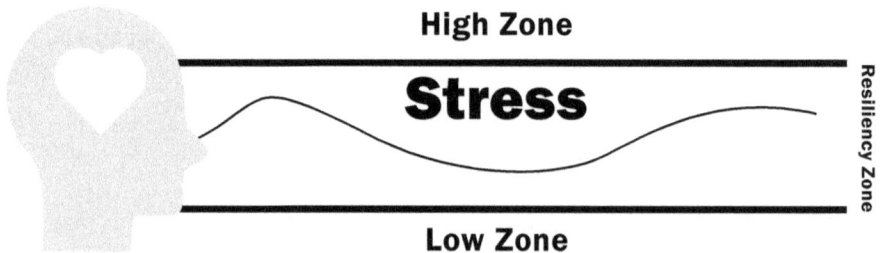

Figure 1.1. The Zone. (Adapted by Elaine Miller-Karas from an original graphic by Peter Levine and Diane Heller, original slide design by Genie Everett. Permission given by Elaina Miller-Karas.)

The Zone is a simple structure, a mental picture of two horizontal lines. The width between the two lines is determined by how you are thinking and feeling, physically and emotionally, at any moment during your day. Typically, when you are between those two horizontal lines and in the zone, you are at your best, happiest, most content self, able to manage stress, make your best decisions, and navigate health care's pain points. Explained another way by Mihaly Csikszentmihalyi, you are in your "flow." He wrote in his book *Flow* that those who can manage their inner experiences are better able to determine the quality of their lives as measured by a feeling of happiness, satisfaction, and a sense of achievement.[2]

If you're having a good day and many, if not most, things are going your way, your zone will likely be wider. The wider your zone, the less likely you will get bumped out. On the other hand, if you are thinking and feeling negative, those two lines will likely be closer together, making your zone narrower. The narrower your zone is, the more likely you may find yourself outside of those lines, either above or below. Given the intrinsic challenges and complexities of health care (and the patients we serve), the width of those lines can change quickly during the roller coaster of a day, based upon your internal thoughts or the day's events and your response to them.

What is it like for people to be in their zone/flow? Here are some descriptions.

1. Feeling calm, patient, focused, innovative, creative, able to think most clearly and be most content. Their bodies might feel light, shoulders down, face relaxed. Time doesn't exist.

2. Being an active, generous, engaged, undistracted listener, and picking up clues from body language and facial expressions. Able to focus solely on what is being said as opposed to just waiting for a turn to speak. Listening with curiosity and avoiding judgment. Listening for the speaker's content, intent, and emotions, based upon the spoken words and the tone, volume, and pitch of their voice.[3] As described by Stephen Covey, "Seeking first to understand, and then to be understood."[4]

3. When it's time to speak, choosing and adjusting words based upon the person they are speaking with, avoiding competing with someone else's story, remaining curious and empathetic in their responses. Saying the right things at the right times in the right place to the right person. Being careful with written words in text messages, tweets, and emails, visualizing how a person receiving these written words might interpret them.

4. When making decisions, using both logic and emotions in balancing the benefits and costs of their choice. Their decisions are heavily grounded and in alignment with what they truly want in life, giving them meaning and purpose each day and with each interaction.

Being in the zone/flow reminds me of a simple saying about the power of the brain: "People are about as happy as they make up their minds to be." For instance, surgeons might be in their zone/flow when they are in the operating room, undistracted, uninterrupted, fully present, concentrating and focusing, or performing surgeries they enjoy and that are going well. Nurses might be in their zone/flow feeling valued, fully engaged with their patients, and performing what they were trained to do, caring for patients who are grateful for their care and getting better. Students might be in their zone/flow when they are relaxed, concentrating, and enjoying the information being taught, grasping the utility of the knowledge, and passing their exams.

In summary, people who are in their zone are more likely to be *intentional* with their words and actions, keeping in mind what they want and what they don't want to communicate with each individual interaction. As Susan Scott said in her book *Fierce Conversations*, "the conversation is the relationship," and good relationships help to keep you (and your relationships) within your zone(s).[5]

Triggered: Not If, When

At some time, we all get triggered. It's not if, it's when. Examples of health care–related triggers may include a computer working slowly, especially when you are short on time; additional clicks in the EMR; being disrespected by a colleague or patient; being unfairly judged; saying something we shouldn't have, or not saying something we should have; making a mistake of omission or commission; having to be patient while waiting for a lab test or an imaging result to come back, especially when the patient keeps asking for the result; being asked to wait on the phone when calling a clinician's office or pharmacy; managing a patient who is non-adherent with their medical routine; working with a family with inordinate expectations about their loved one's future health outcomes; or, in general, doing anything that takes us away from what we really want, which is to take care of our patients without distractions or interruptions. Different people have different triggers, and you can probably list your own, though the result is usually the same: We are bumped out of our zones.

We can be bumped out of our zones low or high (see Figure 1.2). When we are in the "high zone" we are usually short, abrupt, and curt with people, even those we deeply care about. This can make it difficult to focus and listen to others, or we may say and do things we might regret, requiring additional energy to repair the damage. Actions associated with being bumped out of our zones may negatively impact patient care and relationships.

We can also be bumped down into our "low zone," resulting in us becoming withdrawn, isolated, sad, and depressed. Others might interpret this as being aloof, distant, uncaring, and unapproachable. This too could put patient care at risk.

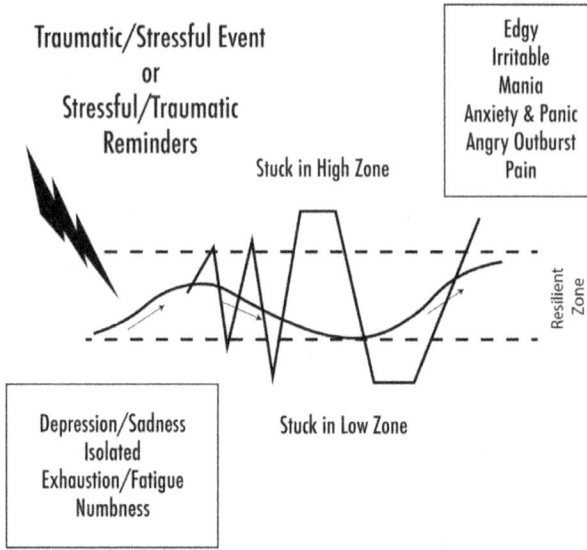

Figure 1.2. Traumatic/stressful event or reminders. (Adapted by Elaine Miller-Karas from an original graphic by Peter Levine and Diane Heller, original slide design by Genie Everett. Permission given by Elaine Miller-Karas.)

Being frequently and chronically bumped out of our zone can lead to burnout, which is at epidemic proportions these days among clinicians and nurses.[6] Christina Maslach, a social psychologist known for her research on occupational burnout, defines classic burnout as threefold: emotional exhaustion, depersonalization (treating people like objects), and not finding in work a sense of personal accomplishment, satisfaction, value, meaning, or purpose.[7]

I met two of Christina Maslach's definitions when I was leaving practice in 2007: exhaustion and loss of meaning and purpose. Sometimes I was feeling so emotionally and physically exhausted by the end of the week after seeing patients all day, every day, working late each night doing my charting, lab and mail reviews, and completing my documentations that by Friday afternoon, I felt so tired that I didn't think I could drive myself home, and I lived only eight minutes away. I also suffered from loss of meaning and purpose. Driving home at the end of long days, I would feel defeated after putting in maximal energy and effort and still having a patient's blood sugars, blood pressure, and lipids be high; or their thyroid blood tests did not fall into place because they couldn't follow or afford their treatment plans; or the insurance companies wouldn't pay for meds or tests. "What am I doing?" I used to ask myself, questioning my personal accomplishments. The one thing that kept me going was the humanity of practicing medicine and treating patients as people without any erosion of empathy. Maybe I had just enough empathy for myself to leave practice before my empathy was completely eroded. If I had known about and practiced the EQ Zone then, maybe I could have remained in private practice and would not have needed to make that change.

In life, there are events that widen our zone and events that narrow our zone. A wide zone may occur when you make a good diagnosis, when you're recognized and complimented by others, or when you figure out a complicated problem. And don't forget about events in your personal life that can spill over into your work life, such as taking a vacation, or being around people you like, or doing things that bring you joy.

For clinicians, some of the causes of a narrow zone are having too much to do and not enough time to do it; running out of energy and being exhausted; seeing patients all day, every day, and winding up with still more patients to see, more operations to do, more charts to complete and more forms to sign. Or maybe you made an error in judgment that injured a patient. Or maybe you are sleep-deprived from being on call the night before, or "hangry" from missing meals during the day to keep your patient schedule running on time.

If you are a nurse, your zone might narrow if a clinician or supervisor admonished you for missing an order, or for not calling them if a patient's status worsened, or for calling them with a "false alarm," or for caring for more patients in the hospital than you believe to be safe, or you are responsible for patients though unfamiliar with their medical conditions. If you are a student, your zone might narrow if you have more to study and learn than time or energy allows, or you did poorly on an exam, or your professor/preceptor embarrassed you in front of the class or on rounds.

Staying in the zone can be hard, no matter how hard we try. The fact of the matter is that we are all, at one time or another, going to be triggered and bumped out of our zones. It's not if, it's when, and sometimes when we least expect it.

Consider this common example that many clinicians in private practice experience. A longtime patient of mine called on a Saturday afternoon and apologetically asked me to call in a prescription to the pharmacy for them, embarrassed that they didn't contact the office during usual business hours. I was in my zone at the time and therefore was happy to do it. I went through the telephone prompts on the automated answering machine, a potential trigger in itself, and chose the one to speak with a pharmacist, since I had a couple of questions before re-prescribing the medication. I was hoping they would pick up immediately, since I tend to be impatient when it comes to waiting. I was put on hold. Then, every thirty seconds, I would get a voice message: "We apologize for your wait; your call is important to us; please hold on; we will be with you shortly." For the first five or ten minutes, I was able to stay in my zone. Then, as the message played continuously and incessantly, I kept reminding myself to stay in the zone and not become agitated, though admittedly it was getting harder to do with each repeating voice message.

After thirty-five minutes, a pharmacy technician picked up the phone. I was still in my zone, though narrower, and explained to him that I had been on hold a long time. He said he would have to transfer me to the pharmacist. I asked him to be careful not to lose me in the system. He said, "Don't worry." That's when I usually worry. Then, just like that, click. I was cut off.

My zone was narrowed further. I called back, waited another twenty-five minutes, and again, a technician answered the call. I pleaded with her, "Please don't transfer me, just hand the phone to the pharmacist." Click. I was cut off again.

I got an immediate call back from the pharmacist, but by then it was too late. Try as I might, I had been bumped out of my zone and went down the slippery slope where I stopped doing my best thinking and behaving. I let the pharmacist know about my travails and she countered by patiently explaining she was alone in the pharmacy with lots to do and not enough people to do it. I suspected her zone was narrow as well. Hearing that, I somehow was able to regroup, get back in my zone, recover my empathy, and apologize, as did she. Our zones widened, the questions were answered, and the transaction was made.

Being Human Is Hard

I wish I could say that I was always at my best self, saying and doing the right thing. Of course, I'd be lying. I'm in the same boat as my clinician and nurse colleagues, exposed to the same demands and pain points, and sometimes succumbing to these pressures. I basically relied on wit and instinct to carry me through when my zone was narrowed or I was bumped out, though there were certainly times that I was not my best self and, afterward, not proud of how I acted. For example, if a patient called the office late on a Friday afternoon, when I was exhausted and crawling to the finish line, and the patient was telling my staff that they'd been sick all week and needed to be seen before the weekend, I'd take care of their medical condition, though with a little less empathy than usual suffering from a bit of compassion fatigue.

I also had Jekyll-and-Hyde moments when I had to go to the hospital in the middle of the night to admit someone from the emergency department (in the days before hospitalists). My wife would hear me blurt a multitude of expletives, followed by tires screeching in the driveway as I drove away from the house. I certainly could have been nicer to the patients at that time, though I was irritable from being sleep-deprived and overworked and consequently out of my zone. An apology the next morning was a usual occurrence.

Shirzad Chamine wrote about the impact of our thoughts on our well-being and life success in his book *Positive Intelligence*.[8] He describes how our mind can be our best friend by using our "Sage brain," which emphasizes empathy, exploration, innovation, and the ability to navigate and activate. Our mind can also be our worst enemy by succumbing to the "Saboteur brain," which, along with the "Judge brain," can inflict self-doubt, loss of confidence, and negativity—causing stress, anxiety, and frustration that sabotages our performance, well-being, and relationships. Your mind can sometimes be your best friend and other times your worst enemy. The hope is that by using the EQ Zone you can more frequently have your mind be your best friend.

Putting EQ into Action

Read the following scenarios and ask yourself these questions: *What do I imagine my zone to be initially in this scenario? Wide? Narrow? How did the change in the scenario impact the width of my zone? How might the change in the scenario have triggered me and bumped me out of my zone?*

1. You are a clinician in the flow of your day, though running about thirty minutes behind in your schedule. Your waiting room is filled with patients who are getting antsy, according to your nurses and reception staff. It's also getting close to lunch time, and you can feel yourself getting "hangry." You are finishing up in the exam room with your current patient when they

begin to tell you a story about a significant loss they recently experienced. They begin to cry uncontrollably.

2. You're a nurse in a hospital or office setting with a patient who is telling you a recent tragedy in their life. It is grabbing at your heartstrings. While empathetically listening to the story, you are hearing another patient who is loudly and wildly yelling, "Nurse, nurse!"

3. You're a student in a health-care education program studying hard for your upcoming exams when your friends, who are not in school, are calling and texting you, with laughing in the background and fun emojis, to come out and party with them.

Chapter Takeaways

1. The zone is a simple structure, a visual of two horizontal lines. When we are between those lines, we are our best selves, in our flow, and others see us as our best selves.

2. Life's events and our interpretation of them can narrow or widen our zones.

3. Our own thoughts can widen or narrow our zones.

4. When we are triggered, we are more apt to get bumped out of our zone, high or low, especially when our zone is narrow to start. It's good to know your triggers so you can avoid them or be ready to manage them when they do occur.

Chapter 2

What Is Emotional Intelligence (EQ)?

*The emotionally intelligent person is skilled in
four areas: identifying emotions, using emotions,
understanding emotions, and regulating emotions.*

—JOHN MAYER AND PETER SALOVEY

After learning about the zone that I described in the last chapter, I found myself assessing the width of my zone regularly throughout my day. Am I in it or out? Is it wide or is it narrow? In one moment, I would feel my zone widen after making a challenging diagnosis, having a good medical outcome, or receiving a compliment. Then something untoward would happen, like my nurse had to leave the office unexpectedly for personal reasons or the lab test I ordered couldn't be done because of an insufficient sample, and my zone would narrow. Sometimes I would be completely bumped out of my zone from an insurance company refusing my request for an MRI scan or approval of a medication, or being far behind schedule seeing patients and knowing that the waiting patients would be upset when I eventually saw them. All this begged the following questions: How did I know if I was in my zone, if it was wide or narrow, or if I was bumped out? How did I know if the person I was interacting with was in their zone or not? How do I make decisions that are intentional to help keep me in my zone? How do I develop and maintain relationships that keep me in my zone and help the other person do the same? How do I know if I am making decisions that are in alignment with what I want and want to avoid?

The answer to all these questions is: emotional intelligence.

Emotions vs. Feelings vs. Moods. What's the Diff?

Before we get into the details of emotional intelligence, let's establish some foundational knowledge about emotions, feelings, and moods. Attendees in my workshops always ask me the difference between these, since the terms may sometimes be confusing and even used interchangeably.

Michael Vallejo, in his article "Emotions vs. Feelings vs. Moods: Key Differences," says that *emotions* are intense, quick reactions to internal or external stimuli.[1] Examples would be the sensation of being ecstatic after achieving something difficult, or terrified watching a scary movie. There has been significant debate as to what is the neural basis of emotions and whether they are associated with neural structures or are neuromodulators such as dopamine (DA), serotonin (5-HT), and norepinephrine (NE).[2] A *feeling* is your subjective interpretation of that emotion, typically influenced by your own experiences and beliefs. Examples could be the feeling of love while being around someone who gives you the sensation of joy and happiness, or hating someone who gives you the sensation of shame or anger. *Moods* are emotional states that are less intense than emotions but longer lasting; they can influence and impact our outlook and behavior. Examples include being in an upbeat mood because there's optimism and hope in our lives, or feeling low and melancholic because we lost our direction, meaning, and purpose.

The value of being aware of our emotions, feelings, and moods, which are influenced by our genetics, culture, lifestyle, hormones, personal growth, and existing mental health conditions, is that they impact our behavior, perception of the world, and how we interact with others. Okay, now we're ready for the main event.

What Is Emotional Intelligence?

At one of my EQ Zone workshops, I asked three physician assistant (PA) students to give me their elevator pitch answering the question "What is EQ?" They gave three different answers and, like the clergy hearing different sides of an argument from different congregants, I responded, "You're right, you're right, and you're right."

All three students were at least partially correct. One spoke about being more aware of how they are thinking and feeling, then making decisions based on those thoughts and feelings. Another spoke about EQ helping us better respond versus react to stressful situations, especially those situations that are out of our control. The third described how recognizing our emotions and the emotions of others enables us to develop and maintain relationships, helping us to be more successful in our personal and professional life. In the practice of medicine and nursing, it's the soft skills, the bedside manner.

EQ is about all of these concepts, and they all start with this basic tenet: Emotional intelligence is the connection between head and heart, logic and emotion. It's **the ability to be smarter with our emotions**, managing them to stay in our zones, through the seemingly infinite vagaries of life that come our way all day, every day. Said another way by Peter Salovey and John Mayer, the originators of the term "emotional intelligence" in 1990, EQ is "the ability to monitor one's own and others' feelings, to discriminate among them, and to use this information to guide one's thinking and action."[3] We humans, at our core, are emotional beings. Susan Scott, in her book *Fierce Conversations*, quoted Daniel Kahneman, a psychologist who won the Nobel Prize in Economics: "We behave emotionally first, logically second. No matter how logical we claim to be, our emotions are the most powerful factor in how we respond and interact with each other. It's not a gender thing or a cultural thing. It's the human condition and costly if we don't get it right."[4] The intent of this book is to help you get it right, and getting emotions right didn't start just now.

Awareness and rudimentary commentary about human emotions began over two thousand years ago when Plato (ca. 438–348 BCE) was credited with writing that "all learning has an emotional base."[5] One of Plato's most famous students, Aristotle (384–322 BCE), then went on to describe anger in terms of being strategic or intentional: "Anybody can become angry, that is easy; but to be angry with the right person, and to the right degree, and at the right time, and for the right purpose, and in the right way, that is not within everybody's power and is not easy."[6]

Approaching the modern era, David Hume (1711–1776) wrote that "the minds of men are mirrors to one another," since in encountering other persons, humans can resonate with and recreate that person's thoughts and emotions on different dimensions of cognitive complexity.[7] In 1909, the psychologist Edward Titchener (1867–1927) introduced the term "empathy" into the English language as the translation of the German term *Einfühlung* (or "feeling into").[8] As early as the 1930s, the American psychologist Edward Thorndike (1874–1949) described the concept of "social intelligence" as the ability to get along with other people.

The modern story of emotional intelligence began with two research professors in the United States, Peter Salovey and John Mayer, who coined the term "emotional intelligence" in an article published in the journal *Imagination, Cognition and Personality* in 1990. This article has become the basis for most EQ models. The authors define emotional intelligence with a model that emphasizes "four domains of related skills: (a) the ability to perceive emotions accurately; (b) the ability to use emotions to facilitate thinking and reasoning; (c) the ability to understand emotions, especially the language of emotions; and (d) the ability to manage emotions both in oneself and in others."[9]

Based largely on Salovey and Mayer's research, in 1995 Daniel Goleman wrote his best-selling book *Emotional Intelligence: Why It Can Matter More Than IQ.* In it, he described five elements of EQ: self-awareness, social skills, self-regulation, motivation, and empathy.[10] Several additional EQ models have been introduced since then with tweaks to Goleman's original paradigm. Though they may use different words, in essence, they are all describing similar if not the same competencies. Consider the following examples from companies committed to teaching emotional intelligence.

BlueEQ is a US company focusing on teaching EQ and psychological safety. Their model includes five skills: self-regard, self-awareness, self-control, social perception, and social effectiveness. Each skill has five additional domains or behaviors. In self-regard, there is optimism, self-respect, self-confidence, motivation, independence; in self-awareness, there is openness, self-knowledge, integrity, monitoring, introspection; in self-control, there is impulse control, stress tolerance, emotional stability, resilience, delayed gratification; in social perception, there is empathy, observation, anticipation, interpretation, mindfulness; and finally in social effectiveness, there is influence, conflict management, relationship management, accountability, and ego management.[11]

In their book *Emotional Intelligence 2.0*, Travis Bradberry and Jean Greaves condense the EQ model into four components: "self-awareness," "social awareness," "self-management," and "relationship management."[12]

Six Seconds uses its KCG model to both expand and apply EQ.[13] The *K* stands for "know yourself," also known as self-awareness. At its core, self-awareness is the ability to identify, recognize, and understand your emotions, thoughts, patterns, and actions (internal self-awareness) and the ability to recognize others' thoughts and perceptions about you (external self-awareness).

The *C* stands for "choose yourself," also known as self-management. Once you know how you think and feel, then you can make the best, most intentional decisions for yourself. According to Six Seconds, to be intentional and make the best decisions, one needs to apply the following competencies:

1. The ability to activate consequential thinking, which is assessing the pros and cons of your decisions. It's logical thinking, which needs to be combined with emotions. In Jonah Lehrer's book *How We Decide*, we learn that the wise person uses both logic and emotions in their decision-making.[14]

2. The ability to navigate your emotions and use those emotions for energy. As an example, you're angry because you are blocked from getting what you want. You can either linger in that anger, suppress it, or blame others. Or you can use that anger to energize you to continue looking around and beyond what is blocking you, not giving up getting what you want.

3. Exercising intrinsic motivation, recognizing what truly drives you, what you really value and are committed to, versus extrinsic motivators such as fame, fortune, power, money, or fear of punishment.

4. Engaging optimism, recognizing that if your decision doesn't work out, you will persevere to find another way to get what you desire. It's reminiscent of the proverbial saying, "You get knocked down, but you get up again." It's that half-full versus half-empty mindset people often talk about.

The *G* stands for "give yourself." Once you know how you think and feel and are ready to be intentional with your decision, you then ask yourself, "Is this decision in alignment with what gives me meaning and purpose in life, each day and with each interaction?" In other words, what do you really *want* to have happen, how might this impact you or the other person or persons (think of the pebble in the pond analogy and the ripple effect), and what do you *not want* to have happen? And maybe even more important: Why do you want these things to happen or not happen?

In the KCG model, empathy is also listed under "give yourself," also known as self-direction. A plausible reason for doing so is that for individuals to achieve their meaning and purpose, they often require the support of others. It's hard to get through life alone. Most, if not all, of us need others to help us through the difficult times. We need to be connected with others. To that end, empathy is a very powerful connector of people.

After studying these individual paradigms, the one I'd like to offer you, since it makes the most sense to me and is hopefully the easiest for you to gain understanding and competency, combines the Six Seconds KCG elements and the Travis Bradberry/Jean Greaves model (i.e., self- and social awareness and self- and relationship management). Combining these two models provides us with this new paradigm: self- and social awareness, self- and relationship management, and self-direction. To help you better visualize these competencies in real time, I added "The Zone" concept as described in Chapter 1, to form the "EQ Zone," which I believe gives additional meaning, value, and a visualized structure on how to apply emotional intelligence every day and with every interaction, when life is stress-free and stressful. The result is a model of emotional intelligence (Figure 2.1) that I believe is practical and easy to learn and use throughout the day.

	SELF	**SOCIAL**
Awareness	The ability to know our desires, motivations, and wants and to recognize, identify, and understand our thoughts and feelings, specifically our emotions and patterns (internal self-awareness) and whether we are in our zone or not. Additionally, it's the ability to recognize how we are perceived by others in various contexts and situations (external self-awareness).	The ability to identify, recognize, and understand the emotions in other people and to know what they are thinking and feeling and whether they are in their zones or not.
Management	The ability to recognize choices and make intentional decisions using self- and social awareness, logic, emotions, intrinsic motivation, and optimism to stay in your zone and keep it wide.	The ability to develop and maintain relationships in one's personal and professional lives to keep themselves and the other people they interact with in their zones.
Direction	Knowing what gives you meaning and purpose and why. Making decisions in alignment with that. Knowing what you want each day for yourself and what you want to avoid with the goal of staying in your zone and keeping it wide.	Knowing what you want with each interaction with another person or group. Recognizing your emotional wake, assisting each person to stay in their zone.

Figure 2.1. Core components of emotional intelligence.

I also want to address the so-called elephant in the room, which is a common question I get from attendees in my workshops: What is the difference between personality and emotional intelligence? My initial response to this question, especially since I have been discussing the EQ paradigm, is to briefly review a couple of common personality paradigms. I mention the Myers-Briggs Type Indicator (MBTI), which categorizes people, not on a continuum but rather into one of sixteen personality types, based on their preferences for extraversion versus introversion, sensing/intuition, thinking/feeling, and judging/perceiving.[15] I then review the "Big 5" dimensions, also known by the acronym OCEAN or CANOE:[16] **Conscientiousness**—disciplined, careful versus impulsive, disorganized; **Agreeableness**—trusting, helpful versus suspicious, uncooperative; **Neuroticism**—anxious, pessimistic versus calm, confident; **Openness to Experience**—creativity and intrigue versus routine and stability; **Extraversion**—sociable, fun-loving versus reserved, thoughtful. Some add a sixth trait: Honesty-Humility, which is the extent to which one places others' interests above their own. Each of these personality traits exists on a continuum, and a person can fall anywhere on that continuum. Once that foundation is laid down, I then go back and answer their question and give an example.

Personality is who we are at our core, our baseline characteristics and traits, while EQ is the ability to manage ourselves and our relationships above and beyond our personality. Said another way, EQ is different from personality in that EQ predicts how well a person is able to use their personality characteristics and traits when handling the emotions of themselves and/or others.[17]

To put more meaning to the explanation, I use the following example. Consider a person whose personality type is disciplined and careful, trusting and helpful, calm and confident, creative and innovative, sociable and fun loving. I must admit, that's a nice set of characteristics and traits to have. This person might come across as being very nice, pleasant, and fun. However, when it comes to their EQ, they might not have it. Say you were telling them a story about some tragedy you experienced. They may be unable to recognize what they are feeling as you tell them your story (lack of self-awareness) and unable to pick up your verbal and nonverbal cues of fear, anger, and sadness (lack of social awareness). Because they lack those awarenesses, their verbal and nonverbal response back to you is awkward, confusing, and maybe even inappropriate, like giggling, showing a flat affect, or even making a comment that has no connection to your story at all (poor self-management), making your relationship with them strained (poor relationship management). They also can't pick up on what you might need and want in this situation, since they might not even know what they would want (lack of self-direction). Maybe you know people like this? I know, as an example, that I have encountered applicants to a job or our college's PA program who are very nice and pleasant, though after listening to some answers to my questions, it's clear they lack the EQ depth that I am looking for to earn the job or the seat in our program. But wait, there's more about the difference between personality and EQ.

Personality traits are thought to be relatively stable throughout a person's life, while EQ, which is a competency, is something that we can get better at with desire and effort. However, in slight contradiction to this theory, a study by Soto and John found that overall, agreeableness and conscientiousness increased with age.[18] There was no significant upward trend for extroversion overall, although gregariousness decreased, and assertiveness increased.

One may naturally ask if there are certain personality types that might predict a higher emotional intelligence. A study published in 2020 assessing 210 medical students in India found that students who were more extroverted, agreeable, emotionally stable, open, and conscientious had higher EQ scores.[19] Additionally, most of the students who had higher EQs were happiest with their career choice and scored the highest on their final test. This later finding is similar to what we found in our PA students—that is, those students who had higher EQ scores had higher grades at the end of their first year.

Now that you have a big-picture understanding of what emotional intelligence is and how it interplays with personality, let's see what EQ looks like in action.

EQ in Action (or Not)

I suspect many who are reading this book can identify people whom they know, personally and professionally, who just "get it," and those who don't. What I mean by "getting it" is they function well, using emotional intelligence to manage themselves and others when the waters are calm, the skies are blue, and the stress levels are under control. However, they also function well using their emotional intelligence when the waters are rough, the skies are stormy, and the stress levels are high. Here are examples (that you may be familiar with) of people who don't "get it" and some who do. Let's begin with the former.

A surgeon who blows up *again*, reacting at the operating room (OR) scheduler because they can't get the OR times they desire. The ER doc who tells an upset patient who didn't receive something they requested, "Sorry you feel that way," only to have the comment gaslight the patient further. The primary practitioner who receives an email from an administrator informing them they won't be getting a bonus since they haven't met their patient quotas, and react immediately in disagreement with a hostile email back to the administrator.

How about a nurse who, seeing another nurse near the end of their twelve-hour shift and struggling to complete their assignments, says to the other nurses on the unit, "See, they shouldn't be working twelves," making sure the nurse hears their comment, then continues to let them struggle. Or a nurse who observes another nurse being yelled at by a patient's family, and who joins in the argument, escalating the situation. Or finally, a nurse notices one of her colleagues about to give medicine to the wrong patient, a near miss, and yells at her, "Geez, what the heck are you doing? You could have killed that person!"

And what about students in health-care education programs? Let's say you're a student who witnesses another student being embarrassed on rounds by the attending physician. Then after rounds you go over to the embarrassed student, smiling, mocking them how it feels to have "a new one ripped." Or you're a student who does poorly on an exam then goes around bad-mouthing the professor and blaming them for lousy questions and poor teaching. Or a student you are working with on a team project is not holding up their responsibilities and you berate them by saying, "Buck up or we're kicking you off the team," then you walk away.

Compare those scenarios with the surgeon who identifies and understands their own annoyance because they can't get their OR times, recalling that what they tried in the past to get those times didn't work. What if the surgeon pauses, and this time calmly, thoughtfully responds, letting the scheduler know that they understand the challenges of meeting all the surgeons' time requests and then asks the scheduler to help them understand where the barriers are for them to get the times they desire, ending with "if things change and I can have those times, I'd appreciate it." Or what if the ER doc recognizes that the patient is upset based upon their verbal and nonverbal cues, apologizes to the patient for not doing what was intended, and, with empathy and in collaboration with the patient, determines how they can make things better going forward. Lastly, what if the primary practitioner sits with the administrator's email for a period of time before thoughtfully responding, organizing their comments based upon what they want and don't want going forward, making their point without making the other person feel defensive and upset.

Compare these scenarios with the nurse who, observing their peer struggling, says to their peer that "twelves are long and hard, and we're a team," and offers a hand to complete the peer's assignments. Or the nurse who observes their colleague being dressed down by an abusive family, goes over to that nurse, puts their arm around them, and calmly removes them from the situation, telling the family that a time out is needed. Or the nurse who, noting a medication being given to the wrong patient, says to the offending nurse, "That's scary. Glad we caught that. We have to look out for each other. Let's review what happened so it doesn't happen again."

Compare the student scenarios with the following alternatives. Instead of snickering and being offensive, you say to your peer with genuine and sincere concern, "That must be so embarrassing. How are you holding up?" Then listen patiently, empathically, for their response without necessarily trying to fix anything. Or instead of disparaging and vilifying the professor, you meet with them and learn more about the reasons why you missed answering the questions correctly and how you can study more effectively. And instead of threatening your teammate with removal from the team, you seek to understand what it is that is preventing them from finishing their assignments on time, and whether they are able to overcome those barriers, possibly with assistance from you or the team.

I suspect that you can come up with other real-life clinician, nurse, and student scenarios exhibiting examples of high and low emotional intelligence. Let's dissect one of the scenarios above, examining the lower EQ responses and the higher EQ responses using the self- and social awareness, self- and relationship management, and self-direction paradigm described above. Here, we'll do some "EQ in Action" analysis.

The surgeon "who blew up *again*" may not be adequately self-aware and emotionally literate enough to identify and recognize their level of anger, especially when it might be of a lower intensity (irritated, annoyed, pissed), when they still might have time to avoid going down the slippery slope of no return when they become livid and enraged. Nor were they able to recognize if their zone is narrow or if they are even bumped out of their zone. They could have used those feelings instead as energy to respond more effectively (self-management/navigate their emotions). They also may not have recalled that they have been in this situation before (recognizing their patterns), and their past and current reaction (lack of self-management) didn't get them what they truly wanted and wanted to avoid then or now (self-direction). In their reacting, they did not stop and pause to recognize what the scheduler's demands and challenges were, nor consider that the scheduler possibly had a narrow zone or was being bumped out of their zone (lack of social awareness, empathy). Nor was the surgeon's response going to enhance their relationship or reputation with the scheduler (lack of relationship management), potentially making it even less likely in the future that they would get the OR times that they desired.

On the flip side, the higher EQ surgeon recognized they were upset, annoyed, and irritated (self-awareness/emotional literacy) before they hit the slope of no return because they were being blocked from something they wanted, and that strategies used in the past didn't work (self-awareness/recognize patterns). They then paused, allowing their emotional brain to connect to their logical brain, able to remain in their zone, and calmly, with empathy, responded versus reacted (self-management), while taking into account the scheduler's situation (social awareness), seeking to understand the barriers to getting the desired OR times, and working with the scheduler to solve the issue. Doing so likely helped both the surgeon and the scheduler to stay in their zone and develop/maintain their relationship and the surgeon's reputa-tion (relationship management), potentially increasing the chance of the surgeon getting what they want and want to avoid in the future (self-direction).

In a more general analysis of these scenarios, it might be safe to say that the clinicians, nurses, and students who had lower EQ responses did not take a moment to check in with themselves and assess how they were thinking and feeling in those stressful moments (self-awareness). Had they done so, they might have been able to name their emotions (emotional literacy), which would have given them better insight into how they would like to *navigate their emotion* and respond positively using *logic, intrinsic motivation,* and *optimism* in a more productive way, including avoiding counterproductive phrases such as, "I'm sorry you feel that way." That phrase may be offensive and can be interpreted as a criticism of the person receiving that comment by implying that they did not correctly understand whatever was originally being told or done to them. This further gaslights the situation and often makes the apologist look even worse. By pausing (self-management), they could have *recognized patterns* from their past and recall responses that worked and didn't work to get them what they want and want to avoid (self-direction, pursuing noble goals). Pausing likely would have given them all the opportunity to seek to understand the other person's point of view (social awareness) and, where appropriate, respond with *empathy*, a powerful connector of people. In the end they would have more likely strengthened their relationship with the other person, short term and/or long term (relationship management), stayed in their zones, and helped the person they were interacting with stay in their zone, all while enhancing their own reputations.

In the scenarios in which the clinicians, nurses, and students had higher emotional intelligence responses, the components of EQ were used more favorably. It's safe to say that all were upset at having their buttons pushed (self-awareness, emotional literacy), likely recognizing that they had been in similar situations in the past (recognizing patterns), recalling what worked and didn't work. With this, they saw the situation from the other person's point of view (social awareness). Then, rather than reacting, they paused, *navigated their own emotions*, and used those emotions for energy to get what they wanted and wanted to avoid (self-direction, pursue noble goals). After pausing, they responded verbally with *logic, intrinsic motivation, optimism*, and *empathy*, to maintain the relationship (self- and relationship management).

As an example, instead of saying, "I am sorry you feel that way," they could have used a phrase that emphasizes understanding, such as, "What you said really helps me understand the situation better. Thank you." Phrases like that often help defuse a conflict situation.

The primary practitioner also used high EQ competencies, though the communication was in writing. They first paused to recognize how they felt and to understand where the other person might be coming from (self- and social awareness, empathy). They were then intentional with their response (self-management) in hopes of maintaining their relationship with the writer of the email (relationship management), which is what they desired long term (pursue noble goals). By being more emotionally intelligent with each interaction, they likely stayed in their zone while keeping it wide and less likely to get bumped out, increased the likelihood of the other person staying in their zone, and enhanced their reputation.

If you are a clinician, nurse, or student and you see yourself in some capacity in the lower EQ portion of the scenarios, don't despair. EQ is a competency that is learnable, and with interest, desire, and using the strategies that are offered in the third section of this book, you will improve. Even if you see yourself in the higher EQ portion of those scenarios, there are still ways to get even better. We all can. As you practice EQ skills, you will likely feel more emotionally confident and act more emotionally competent, even in very stressful situations. Additionally, your brain will go through neuroplastic changes (see Chapter 4) to help you become and sustain being more emotionally intelligent. EQ begets EQ. Over the years, I have witnessed that health-care professionals are very driven, highly motivated, goal-oriented people. If we strive to achieve something, we usually do.

If you are looking to take your understanding of your own emotional intelligence to the next level, to develop a feel for your EQ strengths and opportunities, you can quantify your EQ with one of several organizational emotional intelligence assessments. If you have interest in learning more about these assessments and the value they can bring to you, the next chapter takes a deeper dive into emotional intelligence, using EQ surveys to make the points.

An EQ Nuance

Up until this point I have described how EQ can be used for good to manage yourself and your relationships, such that both parties are able to stay in their zones, each leaving the interaction better than when it started. However, some might use their EQ skills in manipulative ways to get what's best for them, leaving you devoid of what is best for you.

Consider this discussion (argument?) that I had with a psychologist friend of mine. Their contention was that people who are narcissistic and sociopathic, toxically manipulative, malicious, and deceitful can, and often do, have high emotional intelligence, using it to achieve their nefarious goals regardless of the consequences to the people they are coercing. My initial thought was that manipulative people can't have high EQ and, in a relatively low EQ way, I argued back that since they typically aren't empathic and don't use their influence for a positive impact, they are more likely to have low emotional intelligence. If I had been on my EQ game that evening I would have listened to my friend's assertions, sought to understand, paused, and countered with, "This really helps me understand how you are thinking" and "I would like to study the topic more and carry on the discussion with you in the future," rather than taking the bait and engaging in an argument, leaving us both frazzled and in a narrow zone.

After the discussion went back and forth, I investigated the topic the next day—and indeed, I was wrong. Here is what I found. EQ, like many skills in life, can be used by family, friends, colleagues, salespeople, politicians, and frankly anyone in both good and evil, ethical and unethical ways against others. As described in an article by Justin Bariso, manipulators can be expert at sharpening their self- and social awareness skills and can manage themselves as they manipulate you (self- and relationship management) to get you to do what they want (self-direction).[20] Read these three examples (check out the article for the remaining seven) and reflect on a recent or past personal interaction.

1. Manipulators play on fear, exaggerating and overemphasizing certain facts, with the aim of scaring you into action that benefits them, not you.

2. They deceive by hiding the truth or refraining from showing you all sides of the story, such as an employee who spreads rumors with the goal of gaining a strategic advantage.

3. Manipulators will try to take advantage when you're happy. When we're in a good mood, it's easy to say yes to something or embrace an opportunity that might look good without really thinking it through before acting.

On the other hand, high EQ can protect you against being manipulated and deceived, a virtual shield. In a 2023 article entitled "The Dark Side of Emotional Intelligence: Are You Being Manipulated?," which was featured on the website medium.com, self-reflection and social awareness may lead us to feel more in control of our own thoughts and feelings. This in turn shapes our interactions and empowers us to make autonomous choices, free from manipulative influences.[21] To benefit from this shield, it helps to be in your zone.

Putting EQ into Action

Read the following scenarios and ask yourself these questions: *What might I be thinking and feeling (self-awareness)? What may the other person involved be thinking and feeling (social awareness)? What choices do I have to respond to these situations (self-management)? How do my responses impact my relationship (relationship management)? What do I want to have happen and what would I like to avoid as outcomes to these situations (self-direction)?*

1. You're a clinician, and a patient comes to your office upset. A cancer screening test that they thought was supposed to be done in the past never was, and now, years later, they have the cancer. They accuse you for not ordering the test. They are furious and demand an explanation.

2. You're a nurse in the hospital and gave a patient an insulin injection instead of the intended heparin, causing hypoglycemia. Or you're an office-based nurse who called in a prescription for hydroxyzine, a sedative, instead of hydralazine, an antihypertensive, causing somnolence instead of lowering the blood pressure. Your patient requests an explanation.

3. You're a student who spread a false rumor about one of your peers who now confronts you with this situation and wants to know why you did this.

Chapter Takeaways

1. *Emotions* are intense, quick reactions to internal or external stimuli. *Feelings* are your subjective interpretation of that emotion. *Moods* are emotional states that are less intense than emotions but longer lasting.

2. There are several different paradigms for emotional intelligence, though in the end they are all about a person being able to recognize, identify, and understand their emotions and the emotions of others (self- and social awareness), manage themselves and their relationships (self- and relationship management), and know what they want and want to avoid (self-direction).

3. Many of us can use our natural emotional intelligence skills when the stress levels are under control. What really tests our emotional intelligence is how we think and feel, what we do and say, and what we want and don't want when the stress levels are high.

4. If you see yourself in the lower EQ scenarios, or even in the higher EQ but wanting to improve, don't despair. EQ is a competency that is learnable with interest, desire, and practice. Part III of this book will show you how to do it.

5. Personality and EQ are different. Personality is who you are at your core, based upon the Big 5 traits (CANOE— Conscientiousness, Agreeableness, Neuroticism, Openness to Experience, Extraversion). EQ is how you handle your emotions and the emotions of others to form relationships. Additionally, personality traits tend to be fixed, while EQ is a competency that you can get better at.

6. Highly emotionally intelligent people can use their skill to manipulate others for their own benefit. People high in EQ can protect themselves against these nefarious people.

Chapter 3

Quantifying Emotional Intelligence

*The most central, most significant mode of learning
involved in the process of developing emotional intelligence
[is] gaining insight through expanding awareness.*

—WAYNE PAYNE

When patients go to see their clinician with a concern, the clinician typically begins by taking a history and performing a physical examination. The clinician comes up with a list of potential diagnoses, that is, a differential diagnosis. Then, to narrow the differential down and/ or *confirm what they may already know*, the clinician orders additional measurable tests like labs, an EKG, imaging studies, and more. Having these additional quantified results gives clinicians additional knowledge and understanding about the patient and helps confirm the diagnosis. In many respects, this is akin to people seeing their emotional intelligence results quantified. One of the common refrains I hear from people when debriefing them on their EQ assessments is "I thought I knew that about myself already, though now seeing it quantified confirms it."

Data helps drive decisions, and having people—especially competitive, high achievers like in health care—see their EQ scores typically serves as an impetus for them to decide to take action. The next section provides a few examples of organizational self-assessment EQ surveys that are available to help you gain additional insight and take your own emotional intelligence to the next level.

EQ Is Measurable: Assessments

During my EQ journey over the years, I was curious to learn about the different EQ paradigms and assessments of the more popular EQ companies, aside from Six Seconds, namely BlueEQ and TalentSmartEQ. After studying their paradigms, completing their assessments, and attending their introductory webinars, I found value and merit learning more about my own EQ from all of them, despite the differences in their verbiages and assessment tools. I invite you to check them out and see which is the best fit for you. I am hopeful that you may benefit from either one of them.

BlueEQ (blueeq.com) offers a thirty-five-page comprehensive personalized assessment report; an EQ Heat map, which summarizes their five EQ skills and twenty-five dimensions; and a Psychological Safety score.[1] The TalentSmartEQ assessment (talentsmarteq.com) gives a total EQ score and individual scores of the four key components of EQ: self- and social awareness and self- and relationship management.[2]

There are two additional emotional intelligence assessments that are worth mentioning since they are periodically used in EQ research studies. The BarOn EQ-i was developed by Dr. Reuven BarOn in 1997. The assessment contains 133 items in the form of short sentences and uses a five-point Likert scale. The results can be computed into an EQ score on each of the five factors and the fifteen subfactors: Intrapersonal (Self-Regard, Emotional Self-Awareness, Assertiveness, Independence, and Self-Actualization), Interpersonal (Empathy, Social Responsibility, and Interpersonal Relationship), Stress Management (Stress Tolerance and Impulse Control), Adaptability (Reality Testing, Flexibility, and Problem Solving), and General Mood Scale (Optimism and Happiness).

The Mayer, Salovey, Caruso Emotional Intelligence Test (MSCEIT) was developed in 2002 by these academics from Yale University and the University of New Hampshire. Through a series of objective and impersonal questions, it tests the respondent's ability to perceive, use, understand, and regulate emotions, based on scenarios typical of everyday life. In short, the assessment measures how well people perform tasks and solve emotional problems, rather than having them provide their own subjective assessment of their emotional skills.

Given where I earned my emotional intelligence certifications, I am most familiar and experienced with the Six Seconds assessment tool (6seconds.org) called the SEI. With that in mind, I offer you this deeper dive into its workings to give you a greater feel for the value of quantifying your own EQ.

The SEI, Six Seconds' Emotional Intelligence Assessment, consists of a seventy-seven-item questionnaire that typically takes less than fifteen minutes to complete.[3] Participants respond to each of the items along a five-point agree/disagree Likert scale. The SEI is normed to 100. The scoring range is 65–135. The SEI generates eight competency scale scores distributed across three major categories or pursuits: Know Yourself (self-awareness), Choose Yourself (self-management), and Give Yourself (self-direction)—see Figure 3.1.

PURSUIT	COMPETENCY	DEFINITION
Know Yourself	Enhance Emotional Literacy	Accurately identifying and interpreting both simple and compound feelings
	Recognize Patterns	Acknowledging frequently recurring reactions and behaviors
Choose Yourself	Apply Consequential Thinking	Evaluating the costs and benefits of your choices
	Navigate Emotions	Assessing, harnessing, and transforming emotions as strategic resources
	Engage Intrinsic Motivation	Gaining energy from personal values and commitments vs. being driven by external forces
	Exercise Optimism	Taking a proactive perspective of hope and possibility
Give Yourself	Increase Empathy	Recognizing and appropriately responding to others' emotions
	Pursue Noble Goals	Connecting your daily choices with your overarching sense of purpose

Figure 3.1. Six Seconds EQ pursuits, competencies, and definitions.

Each competency begins with an *action* verb—enhance, recognize, apply, navigate, etc.—again emphasizing that emotional intelligence is a learnable competency. Though not shown in this graph, the Know Yourself competencies are typically depicted with a blue color, since blue tends to be a color of reflection. The Choose Yourself color is typically shown in red, signifying stop. Once we know how we think and feel, we can either react at once or stop and pause to think intentionally about a decision. The Give Yourself color is green. Once we know how we think and feel (blue) and pause (red) to be intentional with our decisions, we then choose to make decisions that allow us to go (green), grow, and develop into the best versions of ourselves. Figure 3.2 is an example of an SEI profile, which provides feedback on the KCG pursuits and the eight Six Seconds EQ competencies.

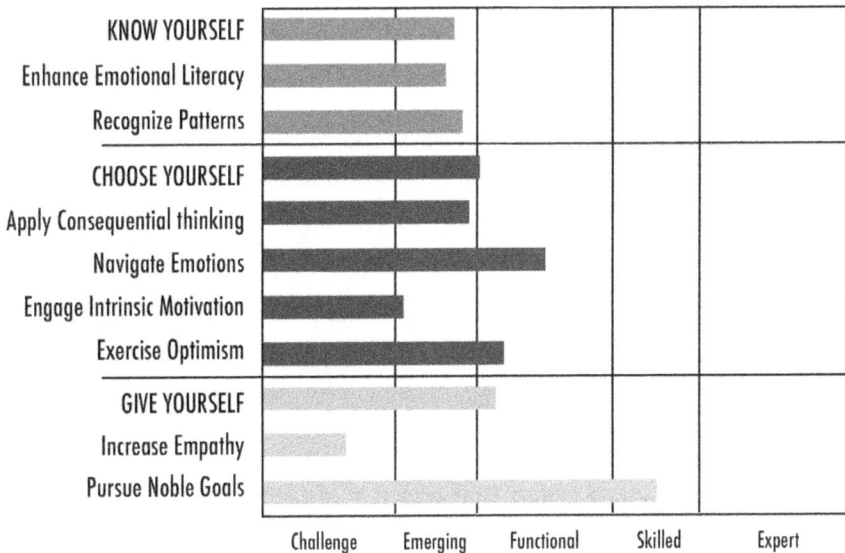

Figure 3.2. Six Seconds SEI profile.

The results can be interpreted in three different ways. One is directional: Some of the bars are longer than other bars, indicating that competency is a strength, while shorter bars present opportunities for growth. In EQ, practitioners generally advise people to leverage their EQ strengths to assist the competencies that require strengthening. Using the above example, if Pursue Noble Goals is a strength, knowing what gives you meaning and purpose, use that as motivation to say, "I know what I want, and I want to get there. To get there, I will need to improve upon my Know Yourself and Choose Yourself scores."

The second way to look at the results is comparatively, that is, comparing one's results to the other half-million–plus people around the world who have completed the SEI in the past. For example, one competency could be labeled "challenge," indicating that a particular competency may be a real obstacle in your life. One could be "emerging," indicating that you are on the path to success in that area. "Functional" means that when the waters are calm, the skies are blue, and the stresses are being actively managed, you do well in most situations. "Skilled" means that when the waters are rough, the skies are stormy, and the stress levels are high, you still do well. "Expert" means that you have a unique ability in that area. People may respond to these comparative results differently. Those with high scores may feel reassured, while some ultracompetitive people may feel they still have to do better. Those with lower scores sometimes feel ashamed, embarrassed, and defeated, though I remind them that I am certainly not judging them. Rather, I commend them for their courage to be open and willing to enlighten themselves about their results, that this is a place to start, and that EQ is a competency that they can improve upon with effort and desire. Others see the lower comparative scores and immediately, without any prompting, take these scores as motivation to improve without me saying anything. Anecdotally, I have found that people in health care are wonderful at self-adjusting once they know their own data.

A third perspective involves examining combinations of the different competencies. Just as in medicine, where we look for *patterns* to make a diagnosis (e.g., itchy eyes, a runny nose, and sneezing with a new cat in the house would be a pattern suggesting an allergic reaction to the cat dander), patterns also exist when assessing the results of the SEI. For example, a high Exercise Optimism score with a low Apply Consequential Thinking score may indicate you are potentially impulsive and open to taking risks. Or the inverse pattern, high Consequential

Thinking and low Exercise Optimism scores, suggests that you are likely overly cautious and may even get stuck with making decisions.

If you have a low Increase Empathy score but a high Pursue Noble Goals score, you might run over people to get what you want, not caring about who you must run over to get it. If you have high Navigate Emotion, Increase Empathy, and Pursue Noble Goals scores, you might be considered a resonant leader, someone who connects and "resonates" well with others.

What would you surmise if you knew your scores were high in Engage Intrinsic Motivation and Exercise Optimism? You're a self-starter or a great problem solver, a can-do person. How about a high Recognize Patterns but low Apply Consequential Thinking or Engage Intrinsic Motivation score? If you have this pattern, you may know your issues but are not inclined to change them.

Knowing these competency scores can help you recognize your patterns and adjust accordingly, so you can make decisions that give you a greater chance of achieving what you want, or want to avoid.

The SEI also gives results on four Success Factors where the overall level of EQ really shows up in people's lives: Effectiveness, Relationships, Well-being, and Quality of Life. Each of these four factors has two pulse points associated with it: Effectiveness—Decision-making, and Influencing Others; Relationships—Personal Community, and Network; Well-being—Physical and Emotional Health, and Balance of Life; and Quality of Life—Sense of Achievement, and Satisfaction with Those Achievements. These factors consistently show strong correlations with SEI EQ scores. In other words, people with high EQ generally show up as being effective, able to build and maintain strong relationships, balance well-being, and enjoy a high quality of life.

See Figure 3.3 for an example of the Success Factors graph. Here, this person is being effective, getting results and influencing others, and maintaining strong relationships but at the cost and sacrifice to their

well-being, balance of life and physical/emotional health, and quality
of life and feeling satisfied with their accomplishments.

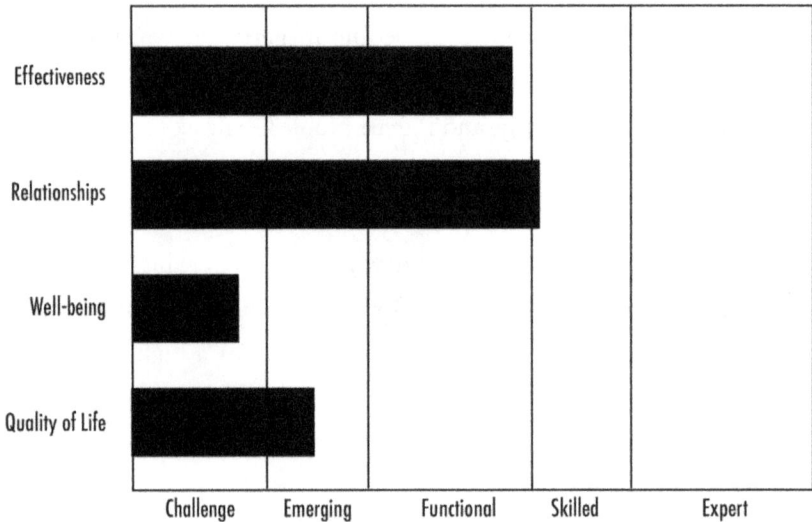

Figure 3.3. Sample Success Factors graph.

EQ in Practice

When I meet with individuals, I emphasize that their EQ score is how
their EQ is at this moment, a snapshot in time. I reviewed one SEI
assessment with a student who had very low scores. I asked her what
her mindset was at the time she completed the questionnaire. She
had been feeling depressed because of circumstances in life that were
negatively affecting her. It showed up on the SEI results. Other times
the SEI reflects one's underlying impression of themselves. One of the
physicians I debriefed also had low EQ scores. I asked him what might
be underlying the scores, and he commented that he didn't think he
deserved higher scores. I found this intriguing since he is the leader
of a major department in our hospital and is well thought of, with an
excellent reputation as an ultracompetent leader and clinician.

I also debriefed a co-worker who was enamored with himself. He had very high scores, reflecting his ultra-confidence in himself, possibly at a level more than others might think of him. It's interesting how one's own perceptions may not match the perceptions that others have of them. This is where a 360-degree review assessment—a tool that compares other people's assessment of the person with the person's own assessment of themselves using the same survey—can help bridge that perception gap. Finally, the SEI gives a Positive Impression score to the person doing the debriefing (in a data sheet viewed only by the debriefer) that alerts them as to the mindset of the person completing the survey. The Positive Impression results are returned as high, low, or average and help the debriefer guide the person who completed the SEI. My co-worker's impression score was high, and I guided him through his assessment accordingly.

Ideally, all the bars in the SEI Profile and Success Factors would be the same lengths, indicating the person completing the assessment is balanced in terms of knowing how they think and feel (self-aware), using that self-awareness to make decisions (self-management), and having those decisions align with what they want and avoiding what they don't want (self-direction). Usually, however, the bars are not equal. I often ask the person being debriefed to consider leveraging their strengths to enhance their opportunities. For example, if you have strengths in Exercise Optimism and Engage Intrinsic Motivation, you can use them to strengthen a lower competency like Navigate Emotions because you are optimistic, motivated, and driven to improve upon that competency. The benefit of doing so, in real life, could be that after you make a mistake, you don't wallow in your anger/shame or suppress those emotions. Rather, you recognize what you truly value (shooting for excellence and not perfection), remain optimistic (I get knocked down, but I get up again), learn from the experience, and plan to do better the next time that situation arises.

Case Studies

Consider these case studies of first- and second-year PA students who were referred to me for behavioral issues and professionalism or who just wanted to learn more about their own EQ (note that I changed the real names in each scenario).

Dave was a young man in his early twenties who grew up fairly privileged in northern California. He was referred because of challenging interactions with some of the patients he was seeing during his emergency room rotation. Most glaring on his SEI assessment was his low Increase Empathy score. When we drilled down on the potential reason for this result, what we found was that he had selective empathy, that is, empathy for some and not for others. The "others" were people who had issues with addiction—substances, alcohol, and nicotine—who were self-sabotaging their health and medical care. Once he became aware of his SEI results, he used his initial anger at the patients as energy (navigating his emotions), reminding himself to take action, and specifically being more empathic. This showed up with him inquiring and learning about his patients' life stories, experiences, and the hardships they endured that led them to addiction. His empathy and medical care for them subsequently grew and improved. As a corollary, he also became more patient and understanding, recognizing that not everyone thinks and processes like he does, including other health-care providers. Possessing this recognition, including being more self-aware, he interacted more patiently with his peers and colleagues, which led to better relationships and enjoyment with being a student clinician.

Sue, a first-year PA student from a rural area in New York State, grew up in a strict home where expectations of her were high and often hard to meet. She voluntarily completed her SEI assessment hoping to learn more about herself, since she wasn't happy about how she was performing in school. She also had a low Increase Empathy score, though hers was not because of low empathy for others but for herself. She had an internal voice, commonly heard among many in the health-care profession, that said, "I am harder on myself than others are on themselves. I have higher expectations for me. I need to do better." She constantly felt like she should have gotten a higher grade on her tests, even though she was a straight-A student. I asked her how she would respond to a friend who was not scoring as high on their tests as they thought they should. She said she would suggest that they give themselves grace and forgiveness. That they be kind to themselves and do the best that they can while learning from the questions they got wrong. I followed up her comment with, "Is it fair to also give yourself the same grace, forgiveness, and also learn from that experience?" I could see her lightbulb click on. She gave herself permission.

Bob was a military guy, with low Know Yourself, self-awareness scores, who got along well with other men who were logical, unemotional thinkers. For those who didn't match his personality and behaviors, that was *their* problem. As it turns out, not all the patients, staff, and preceptors were male military guys, and he was having a difficult time connecting with them. This became *his* problem when he received a failing grade from a female physician preceptor. What to do? Seeing his SEI score helped him better understand his situation. By being more self-aware, he had a better chance to manage his decisions to have him get what he wanted and avoid what he didn't want.

What he really wanted was to connect with people who thought differently, with a diverse group of people, in order to take great care of all his patients. He also benefited from receiving direct feedback from staff, colleagues, and preceptors. With this, he better understood that what he said and how he said it mattered, especially the tone, volume, pitch, and timbre of his voice (enhanced self-awareness). He also improved at picking up on nonverbal cues (social awareness) and recognizing when he wasn't connecting with another and adjusting accordingly (self- and relationship management). He did so well with these changes that he subsequently was offered a job by one of his preceptors. He still had doubts that he would be able to apply these adjustments when faced with the high pressure of the practice of medicine. That's where continued practice of newfound competencies can be invaluable.

Karen, a second-year student in her mid-twenties from central New York, was doing her first clinical rotation in behavioral health. She had a low Navigate Emotion score on her SEI. Low Navigate Emotion scores are common in our own PA students and the general population.[4] I educated her on the value of using her emotional energy to act. In one case, she described working with an eighteen-year-old autistic patient who had PTSD from a car accident. The patient was very anxious and nervous talking to her, which initially made her feel the same. However, she used that feeling to recall that she too was once in a motor vehicle accident, and she became more empathic with the patient. She was also pleased that she recognized her discomfort early. She didn't try to suppress the emotion, which later could have led to an emotional explosion, resulting in her saying or doing something that could have brought her regrets and remorse.

Katie was a kind, caring, compassionate woman, which was easy to discern from her facial expressions, body language, verbal responses, and general demeanor. She had a very high Increase Empathy score and low Navigate Emotion score. She was concerned that she was too empathic and would often take on the feelings of the patients she was working with. The impact would bog her down for the day. We spoke about the value of empathy, using the patient's sadness or fear to connect with the patient empathically, feeling with them in that moment. We then spoke about being smarter with her emotions. By realizing that she would be hearing many other sad and fearful stories, Katie was able to move on to the next patient knowing that she had done her best to connect and comfort them individually, and not taking on the burden of the other person's emotion for the rest of the day.

Derrick was a pleasant and likable yet quirky, nerdy, "young" twenty-year-old who had very high Apply Consequential Thinking and low Navigate Emotion scores. When it came time to make decisions, he was using all his logic and none of his emotions, which got him stuck when it came time to handing in assignments. He ruminated about which literature articles were the best to use for the assignment, causing him paralysis by analysis. He couldn't make a decision, which limited his success in his PA course and could potentially negatively impact him in clinical practice when decision-making is frequent, critical, and consequential. Individual coaching helped him better understand how he was overusing logic and minimizing emotion when making decisions. By more effectively balancing the two competencies, allowing him logically to recognize the benefits and limitations of the articles as well as having him "feel" an article was "good enough," Derrick began to make more timely decisions and ended up completing the assignments in the makeup class and handing them in on time.

As you can hopefully see, EQ is a competency that can be quantified and improved upon with desire and effort, even though some people are more naturally emotionally intelligent than others. Women tend to be eight to ten percent more emotionally intelligent than men.[5] According to a Six Seconds study, Baby Boomers (born from 1946 to 1961) tend to have higher EQ scores than Gen Zs and Millennials, "and as a result form stronger relationships, perform more effectively at work, and achieve higher wellbeing."[6] Six Seconds' explanation for this result is "as people gain life experience, they learn these soft skills are essential to navigating life's ups and downs and achieving personal and professional success." The bottom line is that whether you are naturally emotionally intelligent or become more emotionally intelligent with effort, having high EQ will help you be more successful in your personal and professional life, and there is science to back it up. (More about the underlying science of EQ in the next chapter.)

If you would like to learn more about your own EQ pursuits, that is, Know Yourself (self-awareness), Choose Yourself (self-management), and Give Yourself (self-direction), through the generosity of Six Seconds you can use the link below and complete the SEI assessment at no charge. It can be a great way to begin gaining some additional insight and knowledge about your own EQ.

https://www.6seconds.org/free-emotional-intelligence-test-lebowitz/

If you'd like to drill down and learn even more about your eight EQ competencies and success scores, then I encourage you to contact Six Seconds at www.6seconds.org.

Putting EQ into Action

Read the following scenarios and ask yourself these questions: *What might my own EQ assessment show? How might knowing my personal emotional intelligence scores help me better understand what I am thinking, feeling, saying, and doing?*

1. A patient tells you a story of the significant challenges they are facing in their personal life. Their story is relatable to you since you have had similar experiences in your past. You are now wallowing in that conversation the rest of the day, which is making it difficult for you to concentrate and care for your remaining patients.

2. You're a nurse in leadership who is constantly faced with multiple decisions throughout your day, though you are feeling like you constantly get stuck making the most difficult ones.

3. You're a health-care student who believes that you don't need to study regularly; rather, you feel you can cram the night before an exam and do well. This has not been working out for you, as you continue to do poorly on your exams.

Chapter Takeaways

1. Emotional intelligence is quantifiable and there are several well-validated EQ assessments available. The results of an EQ survey reflect the individual's perception of their own EQ, based upon how they answer the survey questions, and is a snapshot in time.

2. Though these assessments are not a requirement to becoming more emotionally intelligent, completing a formal EQ assessment may bring you great value, knowing more about your strengths, opportunities, and patterns.

3. EQ assessments can be interpreted three different ways: (1) directionally—signifying some areas of strength and others of opportunities; (2) comparatively to others who have completed the surveys in the past; and (3) assessing for recognizable patterns.

4. People with higher EQs tend to be more successful, with the definition of success being more effective, having better relationships, greater well-being, and enhanced quality of life.

Chapter 4

Neurophysiology 101 of Our Fight/Flight Response

Between stimulus and response, there is a space. In that space is our power
to choose our response. In our response lies our growth and our freedom.

—VIKTOR FRANKL

While I was in my outpatient endocrine practice, my nurse would sometimes come into my office during the few precious moments I was not seeing patients, though trying to keep all the balls in the air, juggling charting, returning phone calls, and taking in nutrition. She would then hand me a note from a patient calling into the office and simultaneously, with an aggravated, agitated-looking, and plainly unhappy facial expression, would say, "You're not going to like this." In the blink of an eye between me seeing her facial expression and hearing her say, "Not going to like this," and me saying, "Why," I was triggered into a low-level fight-or-flight mode, anticipating what I was not going to like, a "what now" moment. If I had known about the zone then, I believe this scenario potentially would have narrowed my zone, or even bumped me out of it completely.

In reality, there are plenty of triggers in our professional and private lives that produce common fight-or-flight reactive emotions such as fear, anger, anxiety, aggression, and feelings of stress that can bump us out of our zones and challenge even the most emotionally intelligent of us. Some common examples of triggers may include public speaking; trying to make a deadline; disrespectful, aggressive patients in the office or hospital; realizing you have made an incorrect diagnosis; traffic congestion; or even being on hold or waiting in line for a long period of time, especially if you have a lot to do. I am sure you can think of many more. I've always been intrigued as to what happens inside our bodies that prepares us to deal with triggers, threats, and the resultant stress that challenges our EQ. Maybe you have too. Knowing what happens might give us all more insight and understanding toward becoming more emotionally intelligent. What follows is what I have learned.

Our Fight/Flight Response, Neuroplasticity, and the EQ Zone

In *Discovering Psychology*, authors Don Hockenbury and Sandra E. Hockenbury suggest that emotions are complex psychological states that involve three distinct components: a subjective experience, a physiological response, and a behavioral or expressive response.[1]

Let's use these three distinctive components and see how they play out using a common fight-or-flight situation. Think about when your zones are narrow or you are bumped out, which we all experience to different degrees many, if not most, days and is also what most significantly challenges our abilities to be emotionally intelligent.

Say you have a thought that comes to mind, or one of your five senses (hearing, seeing, tasting, touching, smelling) is stimulated—*the subjective experience.* These thoughts and senses are then quickly and automatically sent directly to a particular part of your limbic system, the thalamus, also known as the relay center, the beginning of the *physiologic response.* The thalamus interprets the stimulus and, if it perceives it as a dangerous, potentially life-threatening situation, it fast-tracks the response to the amygdala, which in turn sends a signal to the hypothalamus. The hypothalamus then activates the autonomic nervous system, namely the sympathetic branch, releasing catecholamines, norepinephrine/noradrenaline, and epinephrine/adrenaline, while also beginning to produce cortisol via the release of corticotropin-releasing hormone (CRH). CRH in turn stimulates the production and release of adrenocorticotropin hormone (ACTH) from the pituitary gland, which in turn stimulates the adrenal cortex, via the zona fasciculata, to produce cortisol.

These stress hormones then circulate through our bodies and stimulate their receptors, which are located on essentially every organ, preparing the body for fight or flight. As epinephrine circulates, the heart rate and blood pressure increase, and cutaneous vessels constrict as peripheral blood vessels dilate, allowing blood to be pushed to the muscles, heart, and other vital organs that will assist the person in fight or flight. The respiratory rate increases, and the large and small bronchial airways dilate, allowing the lungs to take in as much oxygen as possible. Extra oxygen is sent to the brain, increasing alertness. Sight, hearing, and other senses become sharper.

Additionally, still as part of the physiologic response, the catecholamines and cortisol stimulate the release of stored sugars from the liver and muscles, and fats from fat stores, to ensure that the body and the brain have enough energy to sustain themselves during the perceived attack. Insulin production and release is also decreased to prevent the risk of hypoglycemia. Cortisol also slows functions that would be non-essential or harmful in a fight-or-flight situation. It changes immune system responses and suppresses the digestive system, the reproductive system, and growth processes.

All these changes happen so quickly that people aren't aware of them. In fact, in situations of danger, the fast thalamus-amygdala pathway is so useful and efficient that the amygdala and hypothalamus start this cascade even before the brain's cortical/logic centers have had a chance to fully process what is happening. That's why people can manifest the *behavioral* or *expressive response* and jump out of the path of an oncoming car even before they think about what they are doing. In his 1995 book *Emotional Intelligence*, Daniel Goleman called this neurological sequence of events to potentially life-threatening situations a brain 911 alert.[2] Our brains recognize emotions before we figure out how to understand and use them, though eventually we do so. Read on.

During an acute emotional response, the thalamus is also sending information to the prefrontal cortex, the part of the brain that sits right above our eyes and does our executive functioning, for more a thorough check on what's happening (see Figure 4.1).[3] The prefrontal cortex assesses the situation, then creates a more balanced, detailed, and accurate representation of the stimulus as the cortex tries to make logical sense of what our emotions are trying to tell us what to do (action). This indirect pathway is more highly processed and reaches the amygdala after a brief time lag. The cortex then communicates with the amygdala. If the threat is just a stick on the path, as an example, and not a snake, the parasympathetic branch of the autonomic nervous system—the rest and digest system—kicks in and puts the brakes on the sympathetic nervous system's gas pedal.

There is a third option to the fight-or-flight response that is more commonly observed in birds and rodents. It's freezing, a sort of playing dead in the face of danger, though the freeze may also occur in humans who have a "deer in the headlights" response to an acute, potentially life-threatening stress. Freezing manifests as an inability to communicate, react, or take any action of self-preservation or defense.[4] Some may experience this similar reaction when taking a test, or seeing or feeling an overwhelming stress leading to a fight-or-flight reaction, and being unable to recall information/memories or think clearly—that is, the "mind blanking" or "mind freezing."

Connecting our emotional, limbic brain to the logical, decision-making area of our brain (the prefrontal cortex) helps bring understanding to our emotions, identifying and recognizing what the emotions are, where they came from, and what they are telling us to do.[5] For many, making logical sense of that emotion may be relatively easy when we are not stressed and in our zones. However, the challenge for many is how we make sense of those emotions when we are in fight or flight, bumped out of our zones (high or low), when we are amped up, irritated, and agitated, or even sad, withdrawn, and depressed. It's in these situations that we tend *not* to do our best thinking, and there are physiological reasons for this.

Consider the following. We all have a fixed amount of blood in our body. When we are out of our zone, high or low, and our stress hormones (adrenaline and cortisol) are being produced and released, we find ourselves in a fight, flight, or even freeze mode. When this happens, the blood then flows preferentially to the areas of our brain and body,[6] such as our muscles, to allow us to fight or take flight. In doing so, blood flow to the area of our prefrontal cortex is reduced,[7] and in conjunction with stress signaling pathways,[8] logic goes with it. As an example, if I asked you to solve a complicated medical problem or take a high-stakes exam while you were white-knuckling it, driving down a busy, snowy, blustery, slippery highway surrounded by large speeding trucks, you might say/yell, "Not now!" Here is the major point. You just can't do your best thinking when you are overly anxious, stressed out, in an acute fight-or-flight mode and out of your zone because the blood flow to that part of the brain, the prefrontal cortex, just isn't there.

Adding additional context to this concept, I often observe some of our physician assistant students struggle academically then, understandably, become very anxious about passing their upcoming tests. Failing tests raises the stakes for the following tests since repeated failures may lead to dismissal from the program and all the associated consequences. Unfortunately, the more anxious they become, the harder it is for them to learn the information to pass the tests, and concomitantly even sleep, since they are in a state of fight or flight. A vicious cycle indeed, best managed by having the student use relaxation strategies to calm themselves—we offer them numerous strategies on how to do so—break the cycle, get back in their zones, and allow for more normal cerebral blood flow and hormonal regulation, giving them a better chance of learning the material. When we are chronically bumped out of our zones, our cortisol and adrenaline levels are dysregulated, which may negatively impact our sleeping patterns and even contribute to burnout,[9] adding even more to the challenges of learning the material and passing the tests.

Interestingly, a study done on fifty-two medical students showed that emotional intelligence has a strong association with the parasympathetic system (an indicator of higher cognitive ability and physiological competence) and a lower sympathetic responsiveness. The significance of this is that there appears to be an association between activity of the parasympathetic nervous system and a higher order of behavior and cognition. Additionally, higher vagal tone, the activity of the vagus nerve, which is a fundamental component of the parasympathetic nervous system, reflects a greater capacity for flexible engagement to changes in environmental demands.[10] This little extra bit of physiology explains why people with higher EQs can be capable of more successfully managing and navigating life.

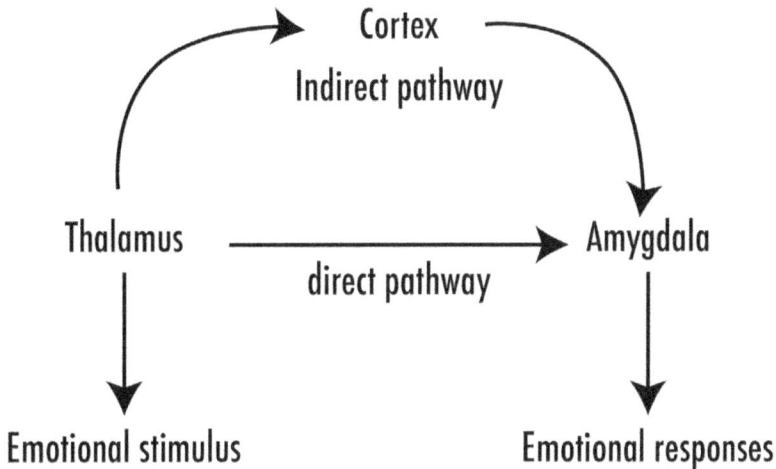

Figure 4.1. Amygdala hijack (with permission from Dr. Joseph Ledoux).

Let's look at a real-life stressful example, where we can apply the concept of connecting the limbic brain with the logical brain, and using the paradigm of a subjective experience, a physiological response, and a behavioral or expressive response. As the senior medical quality director at our hospital, I was leading a root cause analysis (RCA) meeting and, as always, prior to the meeting's beginning, I was scanning the room to see who was there, especially noting any individuals who might make the meeting more challenging and contentious. Looking forward to a smooth, productive session, I felt comfortable and secure that the people who were present were collaborative and respectful.

Then, a person who was challenging, a real button-pusher, walked in. This person was a trigger machine to me. As I saw them enter the room, the visual sense, the *subjective experience*, was relayed immediately to my thalamus, the beginning of the *physiologic response*, which interpreted this person as a threat and sent a 911, fast-track signal to my amygdala, which sent an immediate response to my hypothalamus for stimulation of my sympathetic nervous system and the production and release of catecholamines and cortisol. I was in fight-or-flight mode. In real time, I could feel the blood flow going away from my prefrontal cortex and into my muscles getting ready for fight or flight. Additionally, I felt emotionally anxious, nervous, irritable, and expectant. My heart rate and breathing quickened, the hairs on the back of my neck stood up, I began to sweat, and I had goosebumps and clammy hands. It was a moment of acute stress due to a perceived threat, and it all happened in a literal heartbeat. My zone was narrowed, and I was on the verge of being bumped out.

However, moments later, via the slower indirect pathway, my thalamus connected to my prefrontal cortex, engaging my rational brain, which gave me the opportunity to apply logic and understanding to the emotions I was sensing. Subsequently, I realized I had a choice in how I would respond to this perceived threat (the behavioral response). I could either succumb to the emotions and be hijacked by them and be reactive, bumping me out of my zone, or I could pause, identify and name the emotion(s), "naming it to tame it," using the emotional energy to increase my attention, alertness, concentration, and focus should the meeting become disrupted by this attendee. With that, I calmed myself and could then, figuratively, feel my parasympathetic nervous system put the brakes on the sympathetic nervous system, and have the blood returning to my prefrontal cortex, allowing me to do my best thinking. I was now ready for any hijinks that might come my way and prepared to thoughtfully respond. I was back in my zone. I'd like to think that this is an example of "being smarter with emotions," a term first coined by Josh Freedman from Six Seconds,[11] who encourages people to investigate their emotions to determine what their emotions are informing them to do.

We can also get bumped out of our zone when something great happens. How does that make sense? Imagine you just made a great diagnosis, and your patient is loudly heaping praise on you, your staff, and anyone else who will listen. Or you're a surgeon and you completed a particularly difficult surgery that many would not have even attempted, and your reputation just went up several points. Or you're a nurse and you helped a colleague avoid a medication error that could have resulted in a serious complication to the patient. Or you're a student and achieved the highest mark on the certifying exam or answered a very difficult question asked by a presenter in front of the entire class. You might be feeling pretty good about yourself, and rightly so.

The concern here is that we might be feeling so good that we are bumped out of our zone and begin to feel overconfident, cocky, or invincible. From an EQ standpoint, if we are bumped out of our zone in this way, we might be more impulsive, feel overly optimistic, lose logic, and not consider the pros and cons or risks and benefits of upcoming decisions.

We can also get bumped into our low zone after making a medical error or being reprimanded by a patient or a higher-up, especially if it's in front of our peers. In these situations, we might become over-critical about ourselves, lose confidence, and think that we are a pretty poor clinician, nurse, or student, perhaps even feeling like we don't belong or like an imposter.

I learned both these lessons of the high and low zones early on in my career. I might leave one exam room where the patient was overflowing with praise for me only to walk into the next room where the patient was disappointed or upset with me. One person is willing to give you a slap on the back, the other a slap across the face.

Because of these experiences, my motto was to never let my feet leave the ground, always take one day, one patient, and one problem at a time, keep my guard up, and learn from each experience. The good news is our brains are trainable and neuroplastic, not blobs of tissue that are static. Just like exercising our muscles, we can exercise our brains to make new synaptic connections and improve on our self- and social awareness, self- and relationship management, and self-direction. Our one hundred billion neurons can, and do, make new connections all the time. And just as when one exercises skeletal muscles that can grow, our neuronal connections can grow as well, with the right exercises. By doing so, we can enhance our emotional intelligence so that we are able to think and manage better, even when the heat is on.

I alluded to neuroplasticity in the preceding paragraph. Neuroplasticity refers to the brain's ability to reorganize itself by forming new neural connections in response to learning, experience, or injury. Though early researchers believed that neurogenesis, or the creation of new neurons, stopped shortly after birth, science has shown beyond doubt that the brain is not a fixed, static organ, but rather a dynamic structure that can adapt and change throughout life. Today, it's understood that the brain's neuroplasticity allows it to reorganize pathways, create new connections, and, in some cases, even create new neurons.

There are two main types of neuroplasticity. **Structural plasticity** is the brain's ability to change its physical structure as a result of learning and experiences. **Functional plasticity** is the brain's ability to move functions from a damaged area of the brain to other undamaged areas, for example after a stroke or cerebral event.

Emerging research underscores the critical role of neuroplasticity in improving emotional intelligence by facilitating adaptive changes in the brain's structure and function. Through targeted interventions and practice, individuals can strengthen neural circuits, reshaping the neural pathways in our brains, making it easier to manage stress in the future. In essence, neuroplasticity offers hope and a scientific basis for the idea that we can change how our brains respond to stress, leading to improved mental and emotional well-being.

Moreover, neuroplasticity enables individuals to overcome emotional challenges and develop more resilient coping mechanisms. It's the value of recognizing patterns in our lives. By rewiring neural pathways through repeated practice and exposure to emotionally challenging situations, individuals can build emotional resilience and adapt more effectively to stressors in their environment. Studies have demonstrated that interventions like mindfulness meditation and emotional regulation training can induce neuroplastic changes in key brain regions implicated in emotional processing and regulation.[12] These changes are associated with improvements in emotional awareness, empathy, and effective coping strategies, leading to enhanced emotional intelligence.[13] By leveraging the plasticity of the brain, you can enhance your emotional intelligence and develop the skills necessary for navigating complex social and emotional situations with greater insight and efficacy.

The Pebble in the Pond: The Ripple Effect to Emotions

Have you ever noticed how just one person in a room can disrupt and change the group feeling? Imagine you're a surgeon in the middle of complex surgery losing your patience, becoming agitated as the nurse is fumbling around trying to locate the instrument you requested. Or you're a cardiologist attempting to place a stent in a particularly difficult and challenging coronary artery without success, despite repeated attempts, and now you're starting to mumble some expletive under your breath, though everyone can still hear it. Or you're a nurse at a nursing station talking with an aggressive, belligerent patient on the phone. Other nurses, clinicians, and staff are present as you now begin to raise your voice and harden your tone in frustration. Or you're a health-care student in a study group and you are challenging the members of the group on every question and answer, gradually becoming defensive and exasperated when they push back on your challenges. Your emotional reaction then begins to impact the emotions of everyone in the entire OR, the cath lab, the hospital unit/office, or the room where your study group is meeting. Small mistakes begin to show up; people's tone of voice becomes terse and short as they struggle to manage their own feelings. The reason is simple: Emotions are highly contagious.[14]

Emotional contagion is simply when one person's emotions or behaviors are picked up and mimicked by another person. Usually, these emotions or behaviors happen subconsciously. Fear, anger, joy, and happiness are easily passed from one person to another, often without either party realizing it.

Research offers several explanations for this phenomenon. According to researchers from Harvard University and the University of California, San Diego, happy people tend to be in the center of their social networks in large clusters of other happy people, where each additional happy friend increases a person's probability of being happy.[15] It appears that the muscle fibers in our face and body can be activated without our awareness, and it's those muscle movements that trigger the actual feeling of happiness, in this instance, in the brain.

Other researchers have found that when individuals dislike the same people or find a common dislike of something in general, those individuals have a bond that easily turns into a friendship because it's a connection.[16] Think of the phrase: the enemy of my enemy is my friend.

Research that came out of Parma, Italy, provides another explanation for emotional contagion.[17] Mirror neurons are a class of neurons that become activated both when an individual *executes* a specific motor act and when they *observe* the same or a similar act performed by another individual. In humans, mirror neurons help us in two ways. First, we learn by mapping into our brains what we see around us. In other words, people look, learn, and copy other people's behaviors. Second, the mirror neurons connect us with others' emotions, the basis of empathy. For example, when we see someone smile, our mirror neurons for smiling become activated as well, creating a sensation in our own minds of the feeling related to smiling. This means that noticing and responding to others' emotions are central to our brain's architecture.

Emotional contagion is a phenomenon you can become more aware of, especially if you notice when you have been bumped out of your EQ Zone or if someone has said or done something that has narrowed or widened your zone. Try to acknowledge when you're picking up on the strong emotions of others, and if needed, make a change and adjust.

As a medical professional, I cannot overstate the value of having a greater understanding of what is going on inside your brain and body when the heat is on, the waters are rough, and the stress is high. Personally, I like to visualize the physiologic changes as they are occurring, which helps me stay in my zone. I hope it may do the same for you. Knowing your physiology may help you on your journey to becoming more emotionally intelligent and dealing with the inevitable pain points, triggers, threats, and stress that come your way to some degree each and every day working in health care and even in your personal life.

Putting EQ into Action

Read the following scenarios and ask yourself: *What is going on in my brain and body? Can understanding the neurophysiology of fight or flight better help me manage this situation?*

1. You're a clinician dictating your note on a very complicated patient, while feeling extra stressed with several other patients yet to see, when the EMR system goes down. You are instructed to go to downtime procedures, including putting in orders on paper, though it's been so long since this has happened that order sheets are hard to find. You're also trying to find the labs and imaging tests that you need to care for the patient. You're also concerned that your complicated note might be lost and you have to re-dictate it.

2. You're a nurse, and a clinician just loudly berated you in front of your colleagues for not giving the medication that they ordered at the right time.

3. You're a student, and as you sit down to take your competency examination you suddenly panic, feeling anxious and nervous, with a fast heart rate, quick breathing, and sweaty palms, thinking that you can't remember anything that you studied. You are convinced you are going to fail your test.

Chapter Takeaways

1. We have an entire portion of our brains, the limbic system, dedicated to processing and responding to emotional stimuli including those related to making life-saving and timely decisions, e.g., the fight or flight response when confronted by danger or imminent peril.

2. When we are bumped out of our zones in fight-or-flight mode, the fixed amount of blood in our bodies preferentially goes to our muscles that allow us to fight or take flight, making it more difficult to do our best thinking at those times.

3. The thalamus connects to the prefrontal cortex through the slower, indirect pathway that helps us make sense of our emotions.

4. Our brains have plasticity and can be exercised and trained to make new favorable connections.

5. Emotions can be contagious. Think mirror neurons.

PART II

WHY THE EQ ZONE MATTERS TO YOU

Chapter 5

Making the Case for the EQ Zone

What really matters for success, character, happiness, and life-long achievements is a definite set of emotional skills—your EQ—not just purely cognitive abilities that are measured by conventional IQ tests.

—DANIEL GOLEMAN

One day, I was telling a physician colleague about the EQ Zone. He responded abruptly: "I don't need that." While my colleague is an astute clinician, flawlessly able to diagnose and treat complicated medical conditions, I suspect he may not have fully considered or recognized the value of emotional intelligence, including that it was a much greater predictor of success than IQ—four times more likely, according to a 1996 study out of the University of California at Berkeley.[1] Unfortunately, he was not open to hearing how the EQ Zone can further enhance his professional or even his personal life. Nor was he open to learning more about making the changes that could potentially make him even more successful with an even greater reputation, not to mention helping him manage the pain points to make being a health-care professional more manageable and enjoyable. It all comes down to the old riddle: "How many psychiatrists does it take to change a lightbulb?" The answer: "One, but the lightbulb has to want to change."

In my experience, clinicians, nurses, and students in health-care education programs tend to be skeptical about making changes until we see proof that something truly works. I've come to recognize that there are three elements that clinicians and nurses hold true before accepting something: the credibility of the person telling the story, accurate and reliable data, and self-interest (what's in it for me). Anecdotes, literature, and our own research supports all three when it comes to making the case for EQ and what it can do for you.

Let's start with the anecdotes, since many of us in health care learn best from listening to the stories we tell one another. For instance, a surgeon was referred to me due to repeated confrontational interactions with colleagues and nurses. He was someone no one wanted to work with. Another professional, an ophthalmologist, wanted to improve her interpersonal relationships and manage the disparate personalities to help achieve partnership in her group. In another situation, a couple of urologists were being threatened with dismissal by their practice partners because of disruptive behaviors. What did they all have in common? They benefited by learning more about the EQ Zone and being coached on their personal EQ assessment. When they had all the information, they adjusted and were able to adapt and continue as productive, valuable members of their groups, achieving what they wanted and avoiding what they didn't want.

I also have many anecdotes about second-year PA students who were having challenges recognizing how their verbal and nonverbal communications with preceptors and patients were negatively impacting their professionalism. They faced failing the professional skills course and dismissal from the program. By applying the EQ Zone strategy, the students became more understanding of their self- and social awareness, self- and relationship management, and self-direction. In short, they understood how their interactions impacted their relationships with others, dramatically turning their risk of dismissal into walking across the stage at graduation. Change is difficult, and the common thread in all these physician and student scenarios is the person's openness and courage to change for the benefit of themselves and those around them.

Now let's review the existing literature. Clinicians and nurses who are high in emotional intelligence have greater job satisfaction, higher patient satisfaction and outcome scores, fewer malpractice claims, less burnout,[2] and improved leadership abilities.[3] They contribute to a better organizational culture and climate,[4] which may also lead to improved recruitment and retention of personnel. Additionally, empathy, which is a key component of emotional intelligence, also benefits clinicians and nurses. A systematic review from 2023 reveals that empathic health care personnel enjoy better clinical outcomes, and their patients have more favorable health-care experiences. It also concludes that training can improve individuals' empathy, reinforcing the concept that EQ is a learnable competency, and that organizations would benefit by instituting organizational-level interventions, which are currently lacking.[5]

I've had the opportunity to conduct some of my own research on the impact of EQ in health care in great collaboration with my brilliant colleague, Dr. William Holmes. Dr. Holmes has a PhD in social psychology and is the long-standing research coordinator of our Le Moyne College Physician Assistant Program and a true mensch of a man. Beginning in 2020, he and I began collecting emotional intelligence data on our incoming PA students. Our yet-unpublished data revealed that students with high EQ, specifically optimism, intrinsic motivation, the ability to navigate their emotions, and, most important, experiencing the EQ benefits such as well-being and the ability to develop and maintain relationships, had better grades at the end of the first year, higher scores on their end-of-curriculum exams and PA certifying exam, and more "exceeds expectations" ratings from their preceptors during their second-year rotations.

We also confirmed that EQ is learnable. Students who attended four ninety-minute EQ workshops during their first year in PA school and had only one sixty-minute coaching session on their personal EQ assessment showed statistically significant improvements in their EQ scores and success factors, including more effectively achieving results, enhanced relationships, greater well-being, and higher quality of life. These results were reproduced in a second cohort of first-year students one year later. The improvement in the students' EQ scores was durable and extended into their second year of PA school, even without any additional EQ education. Maybe the most important finding was that the students with the lowest baseline EQ scores had the largest improvement in their follow-up scores, putting them in a position to be more successful when they enter clinical practice.

We also found that students with better relationships were less likely to be dismissed, withdraw, or take a leave of absence from the program or need academic support. As a bonus, based upon the SEI and the Maslach Burnout Inventory (MBI), our data also demonstrated that first- and second-year students with higher EQ and feelings of success scores were less likely to burn out. While our numbers are small, the data is promising, suggesting that emotional intelligence has a benefit on academic outcomes and reducing the risk of burnout in PA students. Ideally, these results should be confirmed with larger studies using the SEI and MBI.

Six Seconds, the international company specializing in emotional intelligence, has data showing that as one's EQ increases, so does one's ability to be successful. Six Seconds defines success as follows:[6]

1. Being more **effective** by making better decisions and being influential by having a positive impact on someone or something.

2. Having good **relationships** with people in one's personal community, like family or friends, and in one's network, like colleagues, peers, or acquaintances.

3. Enjoying enhanced **well-being** by having physical and emotional health and balance of life, however one defines them.

4. Having a better **quality of life** by achieving and feeling satisfied with those achievements.

Travis Bradberry and Jean Greaves, in their book *Emotional Intelligence 2.0*, write that 90 percent of leaders have high EQ and that EQ is responsible for 58 percent of one's job performance.[7] Bradberry also wrote in his book *Self-Awareness* that "83 percent of top performers are high in self-awareness, whereas only 2 percent of low performers possess this critical skill," highlighting that self-awareness is a fundamental and essential basic competency of EQ.[8]

In 2017, El-Aswad, Nadler, and Ghossoub reported on 2,800 physician "star performers" in their book *Physician Burnout: An Emotionally Malignant Disease*.[9] They concluded that 75 percent of the stars' success was a function of their emotional intelligence and only 25 percent was due to their technical competency.

EQ Increases Health-Care Job Satisfaction

According to Medscape's 2023 *Physician Lifestyle and Happiness Report*, the percentage of physicians who were satisfied with their jobs fell from 75 percent before the COVID-19 pandemic to 48 percent in 2023.[10] A 2022 study from Shanafelt and colleagues published in *Mayo*

Clinic Proceedings found that only 57.1 percent of the 2,440 physicians surveyed would choose to become a doctor again, and fewer than half of the physicians surveyed would recommend a medical career to their children.[11] This was confirmed in another study of more than 1,000 physicians reported in the Medical Economics *2022 Physician Report*, in which only 43 percent of physicians would recommend that their child pursue a career in medicine.[12] And it's not just physicians. Nurses, too, are dissatisfied with their jobs. In a survey taken by the American Association of the Colleges of Nurses in 2022, only 40 percent of the more than 9,000 nurses surveyed were satisfied with being an RN, compared with 62 percent in the 2018 study.[13]

As I reflect upon these statistics, I become dejected. I think about how many years it took for me to become a physician: five years of undergrad, four years of medical school, one year of internship, two years of residency, one chief resident year, then finally two years of endocrine fellowship. All told, fifteen years. I know I am not alone. It's taken all of us in health care significant time, energy, commitment, and money to become a physician or nurse, as students in health-care education programs are finding out in real time.

This is where the EQ Zone may be valuable. A study by Nwankwo et al. of forty-five doctors and seventy-one nurses revealed a strong correlation between emotional intelligence and job satisfaction, and suggested that as emotional intelligence increases, job satisfaction increases.[14] Consider other ways that EQ can potentially improve job satisfaction for clinicians, nurses, and clinicians/nurses-to-be. For instance, higher EQ can result in improved interpersonal relationships,[15] team collaboration, and better leadership,[16] stress management and well-being,[17] patient interactions and empathy,[18] conflict resolution, and communication skills.[19] Note that there is a common EQ thread tying these all together: connecting with others by first connecting with yourself.

EQ Reduces Malpractice Risk and Prevents Burnout

There are two additional benefits of the EQ Zone for health-care professionals that are very personal to me and maybe to you too: reducing the risk of malpractice and burnout. I lived through both, and they are likely interrelated.

Consider the following. According to a *New England Journal of Medicine* article, it has been estimated that by the age of sixty-five, 75 percent of physicians in low-risk specialties will have faced a malpractice claim, as compared with 99 percent of physicians in high-risk specialties. Each year during the study period (1991–2005), 7.4 percent of all physicians had a malpractice claim.[20] According to a 2011 CBS News report, more than 17,000 medical malpractice claims are filed against doctors every year in the United States.[21] More recent reports suggest 20,000 medical malpractice claims per year.[22] In the Medscape Malpractice Report 2023, a survey of 3,037 physicians across twenty-nine specialties revealed that 90 percent of general surgeons are likely to have been sued, while 30 percent of psychiatrists are likely to have been named in at least one case in their careers.[23]

I was caught in the malpractice net back in 1998 along with several other clinicians. The complaint against us was missing a diagnosis of pseudotumor cerebri, post-op, in a patient with Cushing's disease. In retrospect, I spent numerous hours collaborating with the patient to confirm the diagnosis of Cushing's, then even more hours with shared decision-making, including getting a second opinion from a national expert on Cushing's to determine the best treatment, which ended up being, for a variety of reasons, bilateral adrenalectomy. As I write this section, I feel myself, emotionally and physically, being re-triggered. What still feels fresh is that being sued was by far the lowest point of my medical career, and this leads to an examination of the value of emotional intelligence in reducing the risk of malpractice. A review of the association between emotional intelligence and malpractice claims "suggests an indirect negative correlation between a physician's level of EI and his or her risk of litigation."[24] The authors go on to say that not all malpractice cases are because of some type of medical error by the practitioner. Rather, claims may be generated secondary to the practitioner's emotional intelligence and their ability, or not, to develop a satisfactory relationship, via good communication and genuine empathy, with their patients.[25] In my situation I had developed a very nice rapport with my patient such that they said that they didn't want to bring a case against me despite their negative outcome. On the other hand, admittedly, I did not have such a rapport with their boyfriend who pushed for the lawsuit which "makes the case."

Managing oneself after being sued for malpractice is another area where emotional intelligence could be beneficial, and where I had opportunity. I did not want to tell anyone that I was being sued. I felt too embarrassed, disgusted, and dejected. This was in line with the Medscape Endocrinologist Burnout and Depression 2024 report, in which upwards of 40 percent of surveyed physicians didn't want to tell anyone about their depression, since it might make others think less of them.[26] This meant that I had to hold it in and deal with it in isolation, which only worsened the intensity of the emotions.

To help navigate these feelings, I tried increasing my exercise, getting enough sleep, and changing my practice location and the amount of time I had for office visits (twenty-minute instead of fifteen-minute follow-ups). I did heavy doses of rationalization, thinking that even if I did make an error, then I just had a bad outcome and was not a bad doc. I also tried thinking positively about all the people I had helped over time, which I'd like to believe far exceeded the number of people I didn't. I also resorted to taking whatever antidepressant we had in the office, too embarrassed to get a formal prescription. They didn't help. It was also one of the first times I had thought about leaving the practice of medicine to avoid ever suffering these horrible feelings again.

In the end, I fought through that very unpleasant moment in my professional career. It wasn't easy and to this day, more than twenty-seven years later, the scar remains. Would I have coped better if I had the EQ Zone strategy that I am using now? I believe the answer is yes. I would have had a go-to structure and strategy to use in real time, beginning with self-awareness, noting to myself that my zone was narrow, or that I was bumped out. I would have been more versed in identifying and understanding where my feelings were coming from and being able to name them. I would have developed self-management strategies that would have helped me widen my zone or get me back in it. I might have had better self-direction, been more intentional with what I wanted to continue to do as a physician and what I wanted to avoid.

I believe going through the malpractice ordeal contributed to my burnout and eventually leaving my private practice nine years after the lawsuit began. My "worried level" and vigilance were higher with each decision, in hopes of avoiding another malpractice situation. It was always on my mind. Research suggests that "a single prior paid claim was associated with substantial, long-lived higher future claim risk, independent of whether a physician was practicing in a high- or low-risk specialty, or whether a state publicly disclosed paid claims."[27] I was probably suffering from some form of PTSD. I was emotionally exhausted. I would call patients soon after an intervention to see if they responded favorably or not, trying to reduce my worry and getting ahead of any potential unintended outcomes. Chronic, prolonged work stressors can lead to burnout, and, to me, they did.[28]

Emotional intelligence can serve as a protective factor against burnout.[29] High levels of emotional intelligence can help individuals recognize and manage their stress levels more effectively, enabling them to cope with challenging situations and prevent burnout.

One key aspect of emotional intelligence relevant to burnout is self-awareness. By being aware of their own emotions, individuals can better identify signs of burnout, such as increased irritability, fatigue, or decreased motivation. Self-awareness allows individuals to acknowledge their limitations and take necessary steps such as setting boundaries, seeking support, or engaging in self-care activities.

Empathy, including self-empathy, another component of emotional intelligence, also plays a significant role in preventing burnout. Being able to understand and relate to one's own emotions and those of others can enhance communication and foster positive relationships in the workplace. This, in turn, promotes a supportive work environment where individuals feel valued and understood. Moreover, empathy enables individuals to recognize when they and their colleagues may be experiencing burnout, allowing them to obtain their own support or offer support and resources to help mitigate its effects on others.

Several studies have highlighted the relationship between emotional intelligence and burnout. For example, a study conducted by Cao et al. found that emotional intelligence was negatively associated with burnout among health-care professionals and that "improving the emotional intelligence of healthcare staff has practical significance in reducing the level of job burnout directly."[30] Another study by Petrides and Furnham demonstrated that emotional intelligence was positively correlated with job satisfaction and negatively correlated with emotional exhaustion.[31] These findings suggest that emotional intelligence can serve as a protective factor against burnout and enhance overall well-being.

In summary, emotional intelligence appears to play a role in reducing the risk of both malpractice and burnout, which may be linked in a chicken and an egg schema. By cultivating self-awareness and empathy, individuals can better manage their own emotions and understand the emotions of others. This can lead to healthier coping strategies, improved communication, and reduced stress levels, ultimately protecting against burnout and the risk of future malpractice.

Let's face it, the pressures of being a clinician or nurse are enormous. The stakes are always high, and one bad decision with a subsequent bad outcome can ruin days, weeks, months, and even years for both the clinician, the nurse, and the patient. We are all human, and invariably mistakes will happen. It's these pressures, affecting a group of high achievers and perfectionists, that raise the incidence of depression, drug and alcohol abuse, divorce, and even suicide among people in health care.[32] How we navigate our emotions and work through these inevitable downturns, errors, and mistakes can make or break a career. Therefore, investing in the development of emotional intelligence skills can have significant benefits for individuals, their overall well-being, and the well-being of health-care organizations. Patients also want clinicians and nurses who are well. Their health "care" could depend on it.

Patients Want Clinicians and Nurses with High EQs

As I was leaving my private endocrine practice in 2007, I curiously asked my patients why they had stayed with me so long. Here's what they *didn't* say: "You made the best diagnosis, you gave the best treatments, you knew the pathophysiology and the disease process, the mechanism of action of all the medications, and oh, by the way, you were smart."

Here's what they *actually* said: "I trusted you, you listened to me, you didn't judge me, you were open and approachable, you spoke directly, honestly, and sincerely, I connected with you, you were kind, compassionate, empathic, and caring." One patient with type 2 diabetes, hypertension, hyperlipidemia, and schizophrenia said to me, "Doc, I think you care more about me than I care about me." The genuine, sincere caring must have worked, since he was able to normalize his

A1C, blood pressure, and lipids, a feat only a small fraction of people with diabetes, hypertension, and hyperlipidemia achieve.

Medical literature corroborates what I learned from my professional experience and my patients' insights. A survey conducted by the Associated Press–NORC Center for Public Affairs Research in 2014 found that out of the top ten attributes patients think make for a high-quality clinician, seven were high-touch elements: listens generously, is attentive and caring, has a good bedside manner and positive personality traits, spends time with their patients, and is a good communicator.[33] The remaining attributes were tech-related: able to make an accurate diagnosis, was competent, and knowledgeable. These results remind me of a famously beautiful quote often ascribed to Maya Angelou: "People will forget what you said, people will forget what you did, but people will never forget how you made them feel."[34]

Patients also benefit from nurses with high EQ by having better outcomes and being more satisfied with their care. A 2021 article from Iran reported a significant correlation between the nurses' EQ and quality of nursing care. Their conclusion, which was in the spirit of EQ being a competency, was to recommend nursing policy makers to institute EQ training into nursing educational programs that would strengthen nurses' EQ and patient quality of care.[35] Additionally, as described in a 2017 article, there was a strong relationship between patient satisfaction scores and the emotional intelligence of nurses working in surgical clinics at a university hospital in the Turkish city of Izmir.[36]

I had a young female patient in our ICU who had Graves' disease, was pregnant, deaf, and lived out of our area. Given her negative experiences with health care in the past, she was very suspicious and untrusting of doctors and nurses. However, one ICU nurse understood her and her experiences, was incredibly patient and kind, worked to overcome the barriers enhancing the patient's trust, and ultimately made it much easier for me to interact with the patient. I lavishly complimented the involved nurse on her amazing abilities. I can provide countless other examples, given the multitude of fabulous nurses I've been honored to work with over the years. It's said that behind every good doctor is a great nurse. I can say with 100 percent certainty that is true for me. I have learned an enormous amount of practical wisdom observing how high-EQ nurses interacted with patients to gain their trust, and while it benefited me immensely, it also gave the patients what they wanted, great care and caring.

One of my mentors during medical school, a nationally and internationally renowned endocrine surgeon, was famous for saying, "Caring without competence is crap." To that, I 100 percent agree. Being technically competent is a must and foundational to being a clinician or a nurse. However, her statement begs the question, "Is competence without caring also crap?" What I learned was my patients certainly needed me to be high-tech, that is, a competent board-certified clinician knowledgeable in the fundamentals of medicine and up to date on all the latest and greatest advances in health care. They deduced I was a competent clinician from talking with other patients, clinicians, and nurses, and reading websites, brochures, or certificates on my wall that showed I had graduated from a reputable, accredited medical school, had a license to practice medicine, was trained and board-certified in internal medicine and in my specialty of endocrinology/diabetes, and that I was annually listed in *The Best Doctors in America*. However, based upon my informal survey, they would also agree with the premise that competence without caring is also crap. In fact, they might be the first to say that what separates the good from the great clinicians and nurses is their bedside manner, their EQ.

Though my patients were special to me, they weren't unique in holding this view. Here is a short listing of the reasons why patients want high-touch, high-EQ clinicians and nurses and the benefits that they receive from them (maybe you can think of more).

1. **Patient Satisfaction:** Health-care providers with high emotional intelligence are better equipped to understand and respond to patients' emotional needs. Empathetic communication, active listening, and the ability to convey understanding contribute to higher levels of patient satisfaction. Patients tend to feel more supported and valued when health-care professionals demonstrate emotional intelligence in their interactions.

2. **Patient-Provider Communication:** Emotional intelligence positively influences the quality of patient-provider communication. Providers with high EQ are more likely to establish rapport, convey information effectively, and address patient concerns. Improved communication is associated with higher patient satisfaction and better adherence to medical advice.

3. **Reducing Medical Errors:** Emotional intelligence is associated with better decision-making and problem-solving skills. In health care, this can translate to reduced medical errors and improved patient safety, ultimately impacting overall patient outcomes.

4. **Clinical Outcomes:** Emotional intelligence contributes to better clinical outcomes through enhanced patient engagement and adherence to treatment plans. Health-care providers with high EQ can motivate patients to actively participate in their care, leading to improved treatment adherence and potentially better health outcomes.

5. **Patient Experience and Well-being:** Emotional intelligence is linked to a positive patient experience and improved well-being. Providers who are attuned to the emotional needs of patients can create a more supportive and compassionate health-care environment, contributing to overall patient satisfaction and well-being.

You may ask "What does a caring clinician or nurse really look like in action?" Consider the following. Patients want a clinician and nurse with whom they can have a relationship, connect, and feel safe. They want someone who generously listens to their concerns with curiosity and without judgment, focused and undistracted, a "loud listener," listening with both their ears and their eyes by recognizing cues from facial expressions and body language. They want someone who is kind, caring, compassionate, who can feel *with* them, someone who responds to their concerns with empathy, and who doesn't one-up their stories by sharing their own story. They want someone who can meet them where they are, who can communicate clearly and directly without riddles, and who is able to distill complicated medical terminology into words they can find understandable and meaningful. If patients are going to stay with a clinician or nurse for any length of time, they want that clinician and nurse to be both high-tech *and* high-touch, competent and caring.

One of my patients made this point painfully clear to me. After I focused feverishly on the care of her diabetes with all the "opathies," hypertension, hyperlipidemia, coronary artery disease, hypothyroidism, osteoporosis, and depression, she said to me at the end of a visit (which lasted forty-five minutes though scheduled for only twenty minutes), "Dr. Lebowitz, you are not smiling today." Her point was well taken. She had noticed my facial expressions and body language. Taking excellent care of her complicated and complex medical conditions was a given and expected, but not enough. She also wanted high-touch.

I also learned a lot about caring from what I called "adult crucial conversations." These are the conversations where I had to inform patients of a bad diagnosis, speak to someone crying because of a significant loss, or had to disclose a mistake I made. I didn't have a structure or strategy to manage these adult crucial conversations where the stakes were high, and emotions ran deep. Especially early in my career, I didn't stop to check in with myself enough to see if I was in my emotional intelligence zone, where I was my best self, or out of my emotional intelligence zone high—stressed and agitated—or out of my emotional intelligence zone low—saddened, withdrawn, and even depressed. In those times, I basically relied on wit and instinct to carry me through. Sometimes it worked out, though other times it didn't, especially during those very tough situations and conversations.

On one occasion, at the end of a typical long and difficult day managing twenty-plus complicated endocrine and diabetes cases and staring at all the charts that were relentlessly piling up on my desk that would require many more hours of my attention, I received a phone call from the grandson of a patient whom I was seeing in consultation for diabetes. He was an OB-GYN resident who pushed hard to know why I wasn't pursuing an evaluation of his grandmother's anemia. At that moment, I became a little defensive. My patience waned, and my zone narrowed even further because I was already tired and irritable from a long, hard day, knowing that I still had more charting to do and return phone calls to make that evening. I didn't take a moment to check in with myself to recognize that I wasn't my best self.

The conversation quickly went south, mostly because of me. I said stupid things that I later came to regret. I think about that conversation frequently, about how I could have, and should have, managed the call and cared so much better. I play it out in my mind and replay what I was thinking and feeling, what I said and how I could have and should have said things so much better based upon what I really wanted in that situation. It certainly didn't meet my goal of giving the best health "care" experience one ever had. What should I have said? Thank you for your call and bringing this situation to my attention. I will reach out to your grandmother's primary care practitioner and have the cause of the anemia investigated further. So easy, in retrospect. Sometimes one must learn the hard way and that phone call, which still resonates with me more than thirty years later, was a big teaching moment for me. Looking back on it, I could have avoided a very unsatisfactory and unpleasant experience if I had had some EQ training during my internship, residency, and fellowship.

(The Lack of) EQ in Medical Training

There is a saying that "what one pays attention to is what's important." The saying was derived from what 1920s researchers called "The Hawthorne Effect."[37] Its premise is that people who are the subjects of an experiment or study to change or improve the behavior being evaluated do so only because it is being studied and not because of changes in the experiment parameters or stimulus. What is not debatable is that I paid a lot of attention during my medical education and post–medical school training to learning to be a technically skilled clinician. I studied relentlessly during medical school—anatomy and physiology, histopathology and cytopathology, biochemistry, pathophysiology, pharmacology, epidemiology, and much more. I was focused and paid attention to what we were taught was the most important aspect of being a clinician: identifying the condition, why was it occurring, and how to manage it, i.e., diagnosis and treatment.

During internship and residency, I put the time and effort into learning each day from my attending physicians and colleagues, skills such as learning how to obtain a history and do a physical exam, what labs and imaging tests to order and when, how to interpret those labs and imaging tests, and how to do procedures such as phlebotomy, central lines, spinal taps, paracentesis, and pleurocentesis. I used "cracks of time" in between cases to read up on patients and hone my clinical/technical skills.

I needed to be strong and resilient, able to work thirty-six-hour shifts every third day after two twelve-hour days. If I couldn't, I was considered weak, and as a result, I couldn't/wouldn't be considered a good doctor. One couldn't help but become *clinically* competent. Being clinically competent was also how I was rewarded in my education and training programs. My reputation and promotions as a "good medical student" were based upon how I scored on my tests and national competency exams. And it didn't stop there. My reputation as a solid intern and resident was based upon my diagnostic and treatment abilities or my abilities to answer "gotcha" questions from our attending physicians on rounds or from presentations that I had to make at morning reports or during conferences. I was honored by being offered the chief resident position and later the endocrinology fellowship that I desired.

Later in my career, I spent seven years as a senior medical quality director at an urban hospital in Syracuse, New York. It was an eye-opening experience. I had emerged from my outpatient private practice isolated, head down, blinders on, seeing patients all day every day, only to do it all again day after day, month after month, year after year. I was a Sisyphus, pushing the rock up the hill each day only to find it at the bottom of the hill the next day.

Being the quality director gave me a chance to come out of my bubble and observe how other clinicians and nurses managed themselves and interacted with each other, with patients, and with staff, especially during the relentless high-pressure moments, caring for very sick people in the hospital. I learned that the challenges I was facing in private practice, managing those high-stress moments, were not unique to me. My colleagues at the hospital were facing the same. I was not alone. We could all do better.

During the time I was a quality director, I sat on the Physician Quality Leadership team and Peer Review Council. Almost uniformly, the cases that came to us were the result of a negative interaction (what we euphemistically called a "communication issue") between a clinician and a patient, a clinician and a nurse, or between clinicians. Communication issues matter clinically since they may end in a bad outcome for the patient. We had examples of this during my tenure as quality director. Once, a patient suffered significant hemorrhaging because there was a disagreement between the interventional radiologist and the surgeon on how to manage a ruptured spleen. Another time, a patient suffered from a perforated bowel after a gyn procedure because the general surgeon and the gynecologist got into an argument over who should be managing the case. To make matters worse, Britt Berrett and Paul Spiegelman, in *Patients Come Second*, explained that if clinicians and nurses caring for patients are not functioning well, it can add to a negative organizational culture and bad patient outcomes.[38] Another reason why clinicians and nurses would benefit from EQ training and putting themselves first, and it's not a new idea.

Galen, the Greek physician and father of systematic medicine, wrote millennia ago (129–216 CE), "That physician will hardly be thought very careful of the health of others who neglects his own."[39] He obviously recognized, even back then, that clinicians and nurses must take care of themselves first before they can take good care of the people who are trusting them with their health and lives. The issue is that many, if not most of us clinicians and nurses, were not educated on how to do so.

Reflecting on my medical training, not once do I remember receiving guidance or strategies on how to manage the inevitable stresses that being a clinician and practicing medicine invariably put on us, other than to be stoic, not showing any weakness lest you be thought a "bad" doctor. We didn't receive any tutelage on how to manage our emotions other than to suppress and compartmentalize them, not letting them get in the way even if it made us come off as cold and uncaring. Facts don't care about your feelings, right? Being emotional could cloud your judgment and logical thoughts. Evidently, our mentors weren't aware of the benefits of emotions in decision-making back in the 1980s. Now, evidence in support of emotions has come to light with this modern claim in a relatively recent medical journal: "Many psychological scientists now assume that emotions are, for better or worse, the dominant driver of most meaningful decisions in life."[40]

I also can't remember any formal education or training that prepared me, or my peers, for what my patients truly needed and valued above and beyond technical competency. It seems that, by chance or how we were raised as children, we just happened to be good at some of the soft skills and had good bedside manners. That was a bonus, but we received no education on how to practice it by connecting with our patients. In his book *Outliers*, Malcolm Gladwell reported that once someone has an IQ of about 120, which many clinicians have, it's enough.[41] Having more doesn't bring any additional benefits or success. What does bring additional success? Being competent in the EQ Zone and having the ability to connect with others by first being able to connect with oneself. Unfortunately, we didn't get this essential and additional EQ Zone training.

Nor did we receive training in how to manage the emotions of our patients, how to comfort a crying patient who had experienced a significant loss or manage a patient who was angry that a mistake was made in their care. We weren't taught how to develop a relationship and trust with a patient. Maybe our mentors just didn't know. Dan Goleman's pioneering book, *Emotional Intelligence: Why It Can Matter More Than IQ*, wasn't published until 1995. Even today, when emotional intelligence has been "associated with better academic performance, better mental health, happiness, learning environment, good sleep quality and less fatigue, and greater empathy" in a systematic review, EQ has not been universally incorporated into medical school or health-care education programs in general.[42]

Sir William Osler was quoted as saying, "The good physician takes care of the disease. The great physician takes care of the person who has the disease."[43] I believe the same can be said about nurses. Not having that EQ education during clinician, or nurse, training may be a significant missed opportunity to assist and elevate our good clinicians and nurses to be great while also teaching them how to healthfully cope through the ups and downs of both their training program and their eventual clinical and nursing practices.

I learned early on that to make it through, I would need to adjust my thinking and attitude. As a relatively new first-year intern, I was covering the ICU overnight where a patient was being treated for diabetic ketoacidosis, DKA. They were on an insulin IV infusion, receiving IV fluids and having their electrolytes measured frequently. I made all the appropriate adjustments to close the anion gap and resolve the acidemia and maintain a euboxic (normal) state. However, the one "small" detail I missed, which wasn't small at all, was not giving subcutaneous insulin to replace the intravenous insulin that I was discontinuing. By the next morning, the patient's DKA recurred. I was confronted with this error in front of the entire ICU team. Shame, guilt, anger, and sadness quickly came over me and the feelings lasted much longer than it took to correct the recurrent DKA.

Fortunately, a psychiatrist friend of mine noticed, pulled me aside, and gave me a life lesson on self-forgiveness. She said, "Are you perfect? Shooting for excellence is good. Shooting for perfection is not good." Sometimes this is hard to grasp, especially when the expectations of our patients are so high ("Doc, I know you are not perfect and will make mistakes, just don't make them on me . . .").

When I was quality director, my responsibility was to help make the hospital safer, more efficient, of higher quality, and more cost-effective. I needed to put in place processes, systems, and solutions to achieve organizational goals such as reducing the average length of stay, readmission rates, complications, mortality, morbidity, and costs. Just like I learned that having meaningful relationships with my patients was fruitful and beneficial, I learned that having solid relationships with clinicians, nurses, and staff also made a huge difference. I spent considerable time developing those relationships and enhancing our organizational culture (what we do) and organizational climate (how we feel about the work we do, since we always do it better when we feel good about it).

How did I do it? Wit and instinct, plus a touch of Dale Carnegie's *How to Win Friends and Influence People*.[44] Though I had no specific strategy, I knew I had to develop trust with everyone. Therefore, similar to how I interacted with my patients, I did a lot of genuine, generous, active, empathic listening. And when I said I would investigate an issue or solve a problem, I made sure that I did and circled back to the individual or the group making sure I followed up, which helped to develop trust.

What grabbed my interest over time with caring for patients wasn't the disease process as much as the person's response to the process and how I was going to respond to their response. How did the person with new-onset type 1 diabetes respond to the news? Did they rise to the occasion, or did they succumb to it? And what was at the foundation of their response? Why were some so much more resilient while others were not? To meet their needs, I had to be a clinician-chameleon, and as the quality director, an admin chameleon, adjusting to people's responses and preferring not to deploy the "my way or the highway" mindset. A systematic review of physicians published in 2022 revealed that doctors with higher EQ appeared to be better able to practice in line with the General Medical Council's guidance on good medical practice, which includes four domains:[45] Domain 1—knowledge, skills, and performance; Domain 2—safety and quality; Domain 3—communication, partnership, and teamwork; Domain 4—maintaining trust. I believe the same criterion can be used to be a good leader. EQ matters again.

EQ Makes Sense and Cents

EQ can even increase success beyond patient and clinician satisfaction; it can have an impact on revenue. How does emotional intelligence make you more financially successful? Travis Bradberry's answer: "The road to higher income is paved with the quality of your relationships. People earn more money as they become more emotionally intelligent."[46] It's not that complicated that people want to be around people with whom they connect well, and they might be willing to pay more to do so. It's good business to build around people who can generate a good organizational culture and climate, which makes it easier to recruit and retain valuable employees.

It is well known that there is disparity in what clinicians earn in different areas of practice and different locations in our country. EQ won't fix these disparities. However, EQ can help bridge some of the gaps. Travis Bradberry, co-author of *Emotional Intelligence 2.0*, conducted a study of more than 42,000 people in all industries, at all levels, in every region of the world using an EQ assessment survey, the Emotional Intelligence Appraisal. In addition to finding that 90 percent of top performers are high in emotional intelligence, his team also found that those top performers earn an average of $29,000 more annually than people with a lower level of emotional intelligence. In fact, the correlation between emotional intelligence and earnings is such that each one-point increase in EQ adds $1,300 to one's payout. Moreover, they didn't find a single field in which performance and pay weren't closely related to EQ.[47]

Compassionomics, a creative book written by Drs. Stephen Trzeciak and Anthony Mazzarelli, emphasizes the connection between compassion and its effect on reversing the cost crisis in health care in addition to the vast benefits of compassion for patients and reduction in clinician burnout.[48] In short, it makes good sense, and good cents, to be compassionate. According to the Carnegie Institute of Technology's research, 85 percent of financial success is due to skills in "human engineering," personality, and the ability to communicate, negotiate, and lead, while only 15 percent is due to technical ability. In other words, people skills or skills highly related to emotional intelligence were crucial.[49] Or as Daniel Kahneman, the Nobel Prize–winning Israeli-American psychologist and economist, has been quoted as saying, "People would rather do business with a person they like and trust than with someone they don't, even if that person is offering a better product at a lower price."[50]

As part of her responsibilities, our PA program director writes letters of recommendation for our graduates who are looking for a job. She showed me one of the forms she needed to complete, which asked her to comment on the following: Does the applicant effectively handle setbacks and disappointment? Do they demonstrate and understand other people's values and have concern for other people's feelings? Can they relate to people from varied backgrounds? Can they keep their emotions in check, even when others are yelling or angry, or accept criticism from others in a calm manner?

Why would employers request such information? Likely because they recognize that health-care employees who have these non-cognitive soft skills make better clinicians, because they have higher EQ and are better able to connect with patients, colleagues, staff, and administration, all because they are better able to connect with themselves. As a result of these connections, they know that the clinician will have more job satisfaction, greater wellness, and less risk of burnout and medical malpractice. Patients too will have more satisfaction and better outcomes. In the end, given the advent of the Affordable Care Act in 2011 and the emphasis on quality versus quantity and value versus volume care, with higher reimbursements associated with patient satisfaction and outcome scores, physicians and others will likely make more money if they have higher EQs. Bottom line, if you want to make more money, EQ pays off.

Putting EQ into Action

Read the following scenarios and ask yourself: *How do the soft skills of practicing medicine/nursing contribute to this specific situation?*

1. You're a clinician, and a longtime patient of yours is now headed to hospice after all available treatments have failed. They want to know if you will continue to be involved in their care until the end.

2. You're a nurse, and a patient of yours complained about your care. Upon reviewing the record, you did everything technically correct.

3. You're a health-care student working in an academic hospital setting with residents and fellows. Some of the patients have specifically asked for you to take care of them in preference to the residents and fellows, even knowing that you are still in training.

Chapter Takeaways

1. The benefits of EQ can be observed in everyday health-care practice and have been documented in empirical research.

2. One can learn about EQ the hard way, examining what worked and didn't work and adjusting accordingly, or, better yet, an easier way is by learning about the EQ Zone and practicing the strategies up front. "High tech" and "high touch" are both important and necessary in managing patients.

3. EQ is a better predictor of professional and personal success than IQ and can reduce the risk of physician malpractice and burnout.

4. EQ increases job satisfaction for clinicians and nurses.

5. Patients prefer and want high-EQ clinicians and nurses.

6. Integrating formal emotional intelligence education into health-care training is still an opportunity for many health-care education programs to assist their students to go from good to great.

7. EQ and compassion makes sense and cents.

Chapter 6

A Deeper Dive Into EQ: Biases, Leadership, Staffing

Emotional competence is the single most important personal quality that each of us must develop and access to experience a breakthrough. Only through managing our emotions can we access our intellect and our technical competence. An emotionally competent person performs better under pressure.

—DAVE LENNICK, EXECUTIVE VP, AMERICAN EXPRESS FINANCIAL ADVISORS

As the old saying goes, "If you have a brain, you have biases."[1] Biases can be defined as an inclination or prejudice for or against one person or group resulting in deliberately held beliefs, especially in a way considered to be unfair.[2] In general, biases are automatic mental processes that can influence our perceptions, judgments, and behaviors. Biases can also be beneficial. They help us make decisions more efficiently. Some literature suggests that we make over 35,000 decisions per day. If we didn't have biases, we would be stuck multiple times each day trying to decide what to do and when to do it. Biases can also produce negative impacts, often leading to unfair or discriminatory outcomes.[3]

I became more aware of the potentially negative impacts of biases as I learned more about their correlation with EQ. Consider this example. As medical director for our physician assistant program and chair of our admission committee, I became intricately involved in our admission process. It quickly dawned on me that I had biases for or against some students just by the way they looked, entered the room, or shook my hand. My biases became even more pronounced during the pandemic, when we transitioned to virtual interviews over Zoom. I became more acutely aware and influenced by the applicants' tone of voice, accent, and even their Zoom background. Malcolm Gladwell wrote about this extensively in *Blink: The Power of Thinking Without Thinking.*[4] In the blink of an eye (about one-tenth of a second), we determine if we trust someone or even like them.[5] Like everyone, I exhibited this response, embedded as it is in our human fight/flight reaction (see Chapter 3). However, I soon found out that the applicants were much more than the way they appeared, entered the room, shook my hand, spoke, or what they chose as their Zoom background. Here is where EQ became incredibly valuable for me and, in turn, for the applicants being interviewed.

In recognizing my biases, especially unconscious, implicit ones, and urging myself to "stop it," I started to give interviewees a chance, to get to know them before drawing conclusions. This worked. When I began asking questions and, more importantly, actively listening to their answers, my biases were frequently unsupported. I made the conscious effort to be aware of my unconscious biases (self-awareness) and then be intentional with my decisions on how to manage my biases (self-management) to get what I really wanted, which was to decide if the applicant would be capable of succeeding in our rigorous twenty-four-month program and become a great PA (self-direction).

I hope you can see in this simple example how using EQ competencies can help you be conscious of and then overcome your unconscious biases. The first step, after accepting that we all have biases, is being self-aware of the width of your zone and your emotions, including how they might be influencing your perceptions and judgments. By being more self-aware, you can also be more socially aware, which involves understanding the emotions and experiences of others. Social awareness can lead to a deeper appreciation of diversity and a recognition of the value of different perspectives. By having greater self- and social awareness, you can be more objective and open-minded so that when it comes to what you do or say in those situations, you are more likely to get what you really want (understanding and clarity) and avoid what you really don't want (unconscious bias and discrimination).

Research has shown that unconscious biases impact the quality of care we as clinicians and nurses deliver. Consider the following examples of bias and prejudice in Jeff Bendix's 2019 article published in the journal *Medical Economics*:

- White male physicians were less likely to prescribe pain medication to Black patients than to White patients.

- Doctors assume their Black or low-income patients are less intelligent, more likely to engage in risky behaviors, and less likely to adhere to medical advice.

- Pregnant women face discrimination from health-care providers on the basis of their ethnicity and socioeconomic background.

- Women presenting with cardiac heart disease (CHD) symptoms are significantly less likely than men to receive diagnosis, referral, and treatment, due to misdiagnosis of stress/anxiety.[6]

A 2016 study published in the *Journal of Clinical Oncology* found that oncologists who rated higher in implicit racial bias had shorter interactions with their patients and had patients who had more difficulty remembering the conversation, had less confidence in the recommended treatments, and were less adherent. Their patients rated the interactions as "less patient-centered and supportive" than patients of oncologists with less implicit bias. The recommendations were to address these biases and health disparities during oncology training and practice.[7] More recently, in 2017, Chloe FitzGerald, at the University of Geneva, Switzerland, reviewed thirty-five articles looking at the correlation between implicit bias and lower quality of care and found all the studies revealed a positive correlation.[8]

Finally, a 2003 Institute of Medicine report on racial and ethnic disparities in health care concluded: "Stereotyping, biases and uncertainty on the part of healthcare providers can all contribute to unequal treatment." Moreover, even White clinicians who don't believe they are prejudiced "typically demonstrate unconscious implicit negative racial attitudes and stereotypes."[9] Maybe Martin Luther King Jr. summarized it best when on March 25, 1966, he said, "Of all the forms of inequality, injustice in health care is the most shocking and inhumane."[10]

In the spirit of helping my students bring their unconscious bias to consciousness and reduce their risk of delivering disparate-quality health care, I ask them to participate in the following exercise. I present a common, potentially frustrating medical case scenario, such as a patient who is repeatedly non-adherent with their medical care, leading to progression of their condition. Then, as I change the patient's variables, I ask the students to be honest with their "gut" reactions, their thoughts, and feelings about the patient (self- and social awareness), how they might manage the case differently with each change in the variable (self- and relationship management), and what they want and don't want to have happen for themselves and the patient (self-direction).

I begin by telling the students that the patient may be a man or a woman, then older or younger, a person of color or White, from

Pacific coast Asia or India, well-dressed or not, wealthy or poor, pretty/ handsome or ugly, tattooed and pierced or not, LGBTQ or not, low body mass index (BMI) versus high, college educated or not. Finally, I give them a choice of common Caucasian versus African American versus Asian versus subcontinental Indian names. We then briefly review different forms of unconscious biases, namely *affinity bias*, where we favor people like us; *beauty bias*, where we favor people we feel are good-looking; *contrast bias*, where we compare people; *gender bias*, where we favor people of one gender over the other; *halo bias*, where we just focus on one positive thing while forgetting about all the rest of the less positive; and lastly, *horn bias*, where we just focus on one bad thing about another person, forgetting about all the other good things about them.

I then ask them to privately consider their thoughts and feelings, since their responses may be very personal. Finally, we talk about where biases and stereotypes (mistaken ideas or beliefs many people have about a thing or group that is based upon how they look on the outside, which may be untrue or only partly true) come from (experiences, beliefs, values, education, family, friends, peers from living life) and the risk of harboring them. I am hopeful that they will recall this exercise, and the thoughts and feelings associated with it, when they are out in practice.

At the end of this bias exercise, as I read the room and notice the skeptical expressions on some of the students' faces that suggest that they still don't believe that they harbor biases, I point them in the direction of the Harvard Implicit Association Test (IAT).[11] Taken directly from the website, "The IAT measures the strength of associations between concepts (e.g., Black people, gay people) and evaluations (e.g., good, bad) or stereotypes (e.g., athletic, clumsy)." This test is intended to uncover biases that people may not be aware of or refuse to believe that they harbor. Though the test may be considered by some to be inaccurate and even controversial, out of curiosity, I took the test myself and was aghast at the biases that I seem to harbor, especially since I thought I was very open-minded. It made me even more alert and conscious of my unconscious biases.

Emotional intelligence can play a significant role in addressing biases and promoting fairness in interpersonal interactions. A 2021 article in the *Journal of Applied Social Psychology* that assessed the correlation between EQ and prejudice showed that those with stronger emotional management skills expressed lower ethnic prejudices. Additionally, high-EQ people have a more positive attitude toward immigrants and refugees and less homophobia. Their findings suggest that "emotion management abilities play an important, but so far largely neglected role in generalized prejudice." This tells us that emotional intelligence can serve as a counterbalance to biases, fostering more unbiased perceptions and behaviors and improving the disparities in health care.[12]

EQ and Leadership

In medicine, if you are a good clinician or nurse, you may be catapulted into a leadership position, like a department chairperson, dean, medical or nursing director, or chief medical or nursing officer. Even though there is some overlap, in general, the skill set to being a good clinician or nurse is typically different than the skill set to becoming a good leader. And that's what happened to me. In retrospect, when I was asked to be the senior medical quality director at our hospital, a leadership position I described in an earlier chapter, I became very excited, and it didn't take long for me to say yes. The attraction was caring for groups of people on a macro level instead of what I had been doing until that point, caring for individuals on a micro level, one person at a time.

Then reality hit. What did I know about leadership and putting processes and systems into place to help our hospital be more efficient, effective, and safe? And there was a lot of reputation and money on the line with Hospital Consumer Assessment of Healthcare Providers and Systems (HCAHPS) surveys, pay for performance measures, Leapfrog hospital ratings, and more. To try to get greater insight and understanding about the position, I met with a prominent dean at a school of health policy who quickly told me I was doomed to fail in my new position and that I wouldn't last six months. I suspect that he too recognized that the skill set needed to be a clinician was generally different from that needed for being a leader. However, when the dean told me I would fail, it reminded me of the naysayers who told me I would never get into medical school. If you want to rile me up, just say the words, "You can't do it." My wife reminded me of this story when I stepped down from my position as senior medical quality director after seven years and left the hospital with the best metric scores we ever had with readmissions, length of stay, cost per case, hospital acquired complications and infections, morbidity, mortality, and more.

How did I do it? First, I recognized that I couldn't even come close to doing it by myself and that I needed buy-in, collaboration, coordination, solid relationships, and an endless amount of trust from my administration, clinician peers, nurses, and staff. In short, I needed to learn how to be a leader and learn the skills that went along with leadership. At first, I did it with wit and instinct, going back to my leadership days playing sports. Then I read all I could about leadership. And finally, I taught leadership to the chiefs of our departments who, like most other physicians, became leaders because they were great clinicians.

What I learned is that emotional intelligence is widely recognized as a crucial factor in effective leadership, particularly in health-care settings where complex interpersonal relationships and high emotional demands are common. Dr. Vipin Jain, in a 2023 article, summarized how emotional intelligence competencies such as self- and social awareness, self-regulation, and relationship management can be valuable to leaders. These include being an effective communicator, building strong relationships, helping with conflict resolution, enhanced decision-making, and inspiring and motivating their teams.[13]

Looking back on my experience, if I had the chance to do it all again, I would have signed up for emotional intelligence training once the medical quality position was offered to me. It would have given me the necessary leadership tools well beyond using my wit and instinct, and it might have expedited the success that eventually came to our organization.

EQ: Recruitment and Retention

As the medical director of our physician assistant program and chair of our physician assistant admission committee, I felt responsible for putting in place processes to help faculty and staff find qualified applicants during our interview process who could thrive in our very rigorous twenty-four-month program and become great PAs after graduation. The risk of getting it wrong was significant for all involved. Naturally, if we chose the wrong student and they failed out, it would be a huge ego hit to them, possibly an embarrassment to their family, and financially costly to the student and to the college. It might also cause our faculty and staff to rethink what we could and should have done better to assess the student for acceptance into our program and to help them to navigate the program's rigors.

Recruiting the wrong clinician to a health-care team can also have significant implications. It takes time to interview, time for the new physician to leave their old practice, and then time to ramp up their practice once they arrive. However, if the new clinician leaves, the practice might have to take on the care of the new patients, overloading the existing staff and increasing their risk of burning out or leaving, and still invest in yet another series of time-consuming interviews to hire someone new. According to an August 2022 article in the *Journal of Hospital Medicine* entitled "Estimating the Costs of Physician Turnover in Hospital Medicine" by Pappas et al., the direct and indirect cost of physician turnover was between $88,000 and $1 million.[14]

Nurse turnover can be costly also. According to a 2021 NSI National Health Care Retention & RN Staffing Report, which included 226 facilities from thirty-seven states covering 144,300 nurses, since 2016, the average hospital has turned over about 83 percent of its RN staff, with the average cost of turnover for a bedside RN at $40,038 (ranging from $28,400 to $51,700), causing a hospital to lose between $3.6 million and $6.5 million per year.[15]

Each percent change in RN turnover costs or saves the average hospital $270,800 per year. The top three reasons for registered nurses resigning were relocation, career advancement, and retirement.[16] According to Marissa Plescia, hospital administrators who turn to travel nurses to make up their nursing shortfall can pay these nurses an average hourly rate of $120, and hiring travel nurses has only gotten more expensive.[17] Travel nurses made an average of $1,673 per week pre-pandemic. Now they can get more than $4,000 per week in some cases. Sumner College calculates that for every twenty travel RNs eliminated, the average hospital can save $3,083,600.

To offset the turnover rates and associated costs, an EQ-focused interview could be valuable in getting it right from the beginning. Adele Lynn wrote about the EQ interview in her book aptly entitled *The EQ Interview: Finding Employees with High Emotional Intelligence.*[18] Hoping to find students with high EQ, we used this book to help us choose questions for our PA applicant interviews who had already been screened to meet or exceed our GPA requirements. Later, after we noted which EQ competencies and success factors were best at predicting academic success in our program, we modified the interview questions. The questions we asked were related to applicants' abilities to develop and maintain relationships, navigate their emotions, maintain their well-being during stressful times, and remain optimistic even when life's events weren't going their way. Just as important as asking these types of questions, we educated our interviewers to listen for specific answers that reveal the applicants' level of self- and social awareness, self-management (communication skills, stress management, adaptability, and resilience), relationship management (conflict resolution, teamwork and collaboration, cultural competency, and their level of empathy), and self-direction. Lastly, we educated our staff and faculty on EQ competencies, since some of our preliminary data suggested that interviewers with more knowledge of EQ, and subsequently higher EQs, may better recognize people with higher emotional intelligence.

You may ask why not use a formal EQ assessment as an additional tool to find the best fit for your organization. The answer is, it's complicated. According to Testlify, a company that helps organizations hire top talent using an HR tech tool, there are definite pros and cons to its usage.[19] On the upside, EQ tests may predict interpersonal skills and workplace success. On the downside, EQ tests can be subjective, lack standardization, raise ethical concerns, and are not the sole predictor of job success. Testlify's suggestions are to use multiple methods like interviews, situational tests, and behavioral assessments tailored to job-specific EQ requirements, and to maintain fairness, train assessors to recognize biases, maintain transparency with candidates, and define clear job-specific EQ requirements.

Retaining clinicians and nurses is another area where EQ can be valuable. Our hospital relies on employee engagement surveys to gauge our employees' job satisfaction. Our last survey was very positive, much improved compared with previous surveys, possibly, at least in part, a reflection of our hospital's new physician- and nurse-led leadership. Leaders set the tone, and our new leadership team brought into play the concepts from Berrett and Spiegelman's book, *Patients Come Second*, by developing a cohesive, collaborative, family-like culture and climate. It also didn't hurt that on occasion, generous gifts and swag were offered to our staff. Based upon the literature, the best possible gift that may be offered to our clinical, and non-clinical, staff is an EQ skill set that can help us all take care of ourselves first, long term. It reminds me of the saying, "Give a person a fish and they can eat one day. Teach them how to fish and they can eat for a lifetime." By teaching our clinical, nursing, and general staff how to fish by learning about the EQ zone, we can better manage, over the long term, how to be smarter with our own emotions and the emotions of others through developing and enhancing empathy and compassion and enabling better understanding of the needs and concerns of our colleagues and patients. Again, we need to put ourselves first.

Additionally, the gift of EQ can help increase the likelihood of staff staying longer at an organization and in health care specifically, by enhancing communication, interpersonal skills, relationships, team-work, comradery, and productivity. In doing so, a more positive and supportive work environment can be created. Consider the following research published by Soft Skills for Healthcare in 2023, in their article "Exploring the Impact of Emotional Intelligence on Staff Retention and Satisfaction."[20] Here are their three main findings:

1. **"Reduced employee turnover":** Emotional intelligence training significantly reduces turnover rates within the organization. Their research found that employees who exhibited high emotional intelligence were better able to address challenges and conflicts in the workplace and, thus, had lower turnover rates. They were able to help build a more positive work environment and experience stronger relationships through their ability to manage their own emotions and understand the emotions of others.

2. **"Increased job satisfaction":** Staff satisfaction levels increased by 20 percent following emotional intelligence training. Additionally, staff who underwent emotional intelligence

training exhibited better conflict resolution skills, leading to improved job satisfaction. By being able to recognize and regulate emotions, individuals with high levels of emotional intelligence can effectively cope with stress and pressures, ultimately allowing them to find greater fulfillment and a sense of accomplishment and experience better job satisfaction.

3. **"Enhanced organizational commitment":** Emotional intelligence training also resulted in higher reported levels of motivation and engagement. Their research found that higher emotional intelligence correlated to stronger feelings of belonging, trust, and loyalty, emotions that lead to increased commitment and engagement and reduce the likelihood of seeking other employment opportunities.

I'll end this chapter with another reference to the book *Patients Come Second*.[21] The authors opine that patients must come second because quality of care suffers if the staff responsible for that care aren't functioning in a culture that lends itself to communication, interpersonal relationships, teamwork, understanding, and comradery. Sounds a lot like they are talking about the benefits of EQ in health care.

Putting EQ into Action

Read the following scenarios and ask yourself: *How might my unconscious biases influence my decisions in these specific situations?*

1. You're a clinician caring for a patient who is heavily tattooed and has multiple piercings. They are complaining of 8/10 abdominal pain and wince as you examine their belly. They are requesting narcotic pain meds.

2. You're a nurse leader interviewing nurses to join your team. One of the applicants is very well spoken, giving thoughtful answers, and could be a good fit for your team though their appearance is messy.

3. You're a health-care student who is graduating from your program and now have several job opportunities from which to choose. One is in an inner city with many impoverished people and people of color. Another is in an affluent suburb with many educated people, and the last is in a rural area populated mainly by farmers and blue-collar workers.

Chapter Takeaways

1. EQ, and specifically self-awareness, can help you be more conscious of your unconscious biases. Clinicians and nurses with higher EQ can reduce the disparity in health care and positively impact the quality of care they deliver.

2. EQ is widely recognized as a crucial factor in effective leadership, particularly in health-care settings where complex interpersonal relationships and high emotional demands are common.

3. EQ interviews can help your health-care organization recruit the clinicians and nurses who best fit your culture and climate and then enhance it further.

4. EQ can help retain clinicians and nurses at your organization by enhancing communication, interpersonal skills, relationships, teamwork, comradery, and productivity, thereby leading to reduced employee turnover, increased job satisfaction, and increased organization commitment.

PART III

HOW TO USE THE EQ ZONE IN HEALTH CARE

Chapter 7

Self-Awareness

When awareness is brought to an emotion,
power is brought to your life.

—TARA MEYER-ROBSON

At the beginning of my workshop on self-awareness, I ask the attendees to raise their hands if they can articulate exactly how they are feeling in the moment. Would you be one of the hand-raisers if I asked you how you are feeling at this specific moment? Typically, only a smattering of hands go up. Then, when I ask one of the hand-raisers what they are feeling in that moment, they struggle to come up with the words that most specifically and accurately reflect their emotion.

Though self-awareness is fundamental and foundational to knowing how you think and feel and whether you are in your zone or not, this skill is not that common. In his book *Self-Awareness: The Hidden Driver of Success and Satisfaction*, Travis Bradberry described the results of surveying 500,000 people as part of his TalentSmartEQ study:

- Only 29 percent of people tested possessed a solid under-standing of their own tendencies, resulting in uncertainty in how they come across to others.

- More than 70 percent of those tested had considerable difficulty managing the stress of interpersonal conflict that is fostered by this lack of self-awareness.

- As self-awareness increases, people's satisfaction with life skyrockets, as they are far more likely to reach their personal and professional goals.[1]

What Is and Isn't Self-Awareness?

Before asking workshop attendees for examples of good self-awareness, it's fun to ask for examples of poor self-awareness. Here are some of the things that they came up with: people who are impulsive, overreact, always blame others, don't accept feedback, and feel like they are always right. They weren't done. People who talk incessantly, not recognizing that they have been going on way too long; people who don't recognize personal boundaries, who literally talk in your face and maintain that close space even when you step back; people who walk close to you and maintain that close distance even when you try to move away and create space; loud talkers, especially on planes or in restaurants, who don't recognize that their voice is traveling way beyond the person they are speaking to. You can probably think of many more examples.

Recognizing what self-awareness isn't may make it easier to define what it is. Self-awareness is knowing our desires, motivations, wants, and needs. It's also the ability to recognize, identify, and understand our thoughts and feelings, specifically our emotions and patterns (internal self-awareness) and whether we are in our zone or not. Additionally, it's the ability to recognize how we are perceived by others in various contexts and situations, which can be very valuable in helping us survive and thrive in a variety of social and professional situations (external self-awareness).

One of our PA students missed picking up on these external self-awareness cues from one of their preceptors when they weren't performing at a satisfactory level. This was a misstep, since they didn't have any formal feedback during their rotation and only found out that they weren't perceived well until the end of their rotation, when they didn't receive a passing grade. When I queried the student about this, they mentioned that, in retrospect, the preceptor had checked out, distancing themself from the student, remaining quiet and not offering any meaningful interactions. If the student had to do it again, they would have taken action after picking up on these cues and discussed the situation with their preceptor in real time, possibly offsetting a surprise failing grade at the end of the rotation.

Perhaps most important to being self-aware, as described by Debbie Ford, the author of best-selling books in the field of personal transformation and human potential, is "the ability to take an honest look at your life without attachment to it being wrong or right."[2] In this regard I ask my students for examples of "taking an honest look at their life and without attachment to it being wrong or right." Here is what they offered: pursuing a career path they genuinely want instead of doing it because of outside pressures; being in a relationship that truly makes them feel good instead of one that looks good; admitting they were the cause of a problem that arose in their life and not blaming their circumstances on others; not recognizing or admitting that their zone is narrow or that they are bumped out and making a big decision regardless; recognizing that how they feel about someone might not be how the other person feels about them. This last comment is another example of being externally self-aware.

On a personal level, when I was on my medical journey, I was using the value of honest self-awareness before I was even familiar with the term *self-awareness*. Consider these highlight moments: I stayed in Syracuse to complete my endocrine fellowship and practice because it felt good to me to do so, based upon the knowledge and reputation of the endocrine professors, the types of challenging diseases endocrinology offered, my attraction to the pathophysiology, and the location of Syracuse, a great affordable place to raise a family. I increased the length of time my follow-up and new consultation appointments lasted because it didn't feel right to me or to the patients to rush them through an office visit. I twice changed where I practiced medicine and eventually left because I felt the way I was trying to practice in the current health-care system was unsustainable (a gut-wrenching decision that I wrote about extensively in my book *Losing My Patience*).[3] Looking back, if I had ignored or didn't take the time to recognize how I was feeling, maybe I would have stayed in practice, likely to my detriment, especially without the benefit of knowing about the EQ zone. However, taking time for honest self-reflection and being self-aware helped me make decisions that in the end were beneficial to me.

What Are You Thinking and Feeling? Check In.

One of the best ways to reap the benefits of self-awareness is to do something very simple. It's called the "check-in," as in, pause and check in with yourself. It only takes a moment. You don't have to sit by a river meditating for endless hours (not that there's anything wrong with that) to know if you are in your zone. Take this example: You must tell a favorite patient that they have a "bad diagnosis." Since EQ begins with self-awareness, the first step is to check in with yourself: How are you thinking and feeling prior to telling your patient this information? Are you sad that the prognosis is unfavorable? Afraid of how they might respond? Guilty that it might have taken you longer than you would have liked to come up with the diagnosis, which might have affected the prognosis? Happy that you came up with the correct diagnosis? Thoughtful about how they might be thinking of you as you tell them about their diagnosis? And what is the intensity of these feelings? The only way to know the answers to these questions is to pause and check in with yourself. Your answer will likely impact what you say or do.

Some clinicians and nurses check in with themselves when they are walking between patients' exam rooms. Others do so when they put their hand on the doorknob, using it as a reminder or prompt to check in with themselves before walking in to see their patients. Clinicians might do so in the privacy of their office, and nurses might do so while sitting at the nurses' station or in the break room. Students might do so between classes, during breaks in the classes, or in a low-traffic area at their school. Some check in with themselves when they are getting ready to start their day, or when they are driving to work or school, or taking a coffee, lunch, or bio break. It's very personal and very effective and, given the roller coaster of the typical days in health care, it can be most valuable if done multiple times during the day.

In a typical day as a health-care professional, you may go from a patient who is eternally grateful for the wonderful care you've given them and how you "saved their life" to another person who is angry that you made a mistake or kept them waiting too long, or who had to pay for parking. This could be followed by a patient who is apologetic for not following your instructions and another who is crying uncontrollably due to a significant loss. The days are not in a straight line, rather a roller-coaster ride. There are peaks and valleys, highs and lows, twists and turns, and the only way to know if you are in your zone is to check in.

One of my diabetes nurse practitioners found this out the hard way. She went into the hospital room of a disgruntled, irritable, "button-pusher" patient who had frequent readmissions for diabetic ketoacidosis due mostly to his non-compliance with his insulin and diabetes regimen.

Immediately upon entering the room, she began reading him the riot act about how his actions were sabotaging his health. He didn't take kindly to her approach and reacted strongly, culminating in throwing her out of the room. After she informed me of the unpleasant details, I asked her what she was thinking and feeling before she went into the room. In essence, she was amped up and agitated, anticipating serious pushback and a verbal fight, in addition to some other personal challenges she was facing at the hospital and in her personal life. In retrospect, her zone was narrow or maybe she was even bumped out of her zone before entering the room, which increased the likelihood of an unpleasant exchange. She and I chatted about this afterward, emphasizing the value of checking in and knowing if you're in your zone or not, and having it as wide as possible prior to entering a patient's room, especially one where the interaction is anticipated to be challenging. She admitted that if she had to do it again, she would have waited to go into that room until she was in her zone, and it was as wide as possible. This is the moral of the story. The check-in is the antidote to being on autopilot and might be one of the most valuable and effective tools you can use to be in control of yourself, the one thing you *can* control. The check-in is a deliberate action. In general, people who may not check in often enough, or at all, will not benefit from the power of self-awareness. Here's the good news. Recall that EQ is a competency, and anyone can get better at it with effort, desire, and practice.

Self-Awareness and Emotional Literacy

Not infrequently, I am asked, "How are you feeling?" about some life event that just occurred. Prior to learning more about emotional intelligence and the value of emotions, I would joke and respond, "What are my choices?" According to Bradberry and Greaves, there are five basic emotions to choose from: "happiness, sadness, anger, fear, and shame."[4] If you are looking for more, the Plutchik model, developed by psychologist Robert Plutchik, has eight: anger, fear, sadness, disgust, surprise, anticipation, trust, and joy, embedded into an Emotion Wheel.[5] The wheel helps categorize and classify human feelings for the purpose of better understanding, labeling, and communicating one's emotional state to others.

So, what does it mean when I am sad, angry, happy, ashamed, or afraid? The following are simple definitions of Bradberry and Greaves's five basic emotions, with an assist from Six Seconds.[6]

> **Sadness:** Something/Someone that you love is going away.
>
> **Happiness:** Something/Someone that you want to continue.
>
> **Anger:** Being blocked from something that you want.
>
> **Fear:** The risk of losing something that's important to you.
>
> **Shame:** Anger turned inward, the gap between what you did or said and what you should have done or said.

Knowing these five basic emotions, or the eight emotions in the Plutchik model, may not be specific enough to truly articulate what you are feeling. To use a medical example, it's like saying "I have cancer" or "heart disease." It's too broad. Similarly, when one says they are angry, how angry are they? Livid and enraged, or irritated, annoyed, perturbed, or frustrated? Or if someone says they are happy, are they ecstatic and exuberant, or satisfied and content? In short, what is the intensity of the anger or happiness so one can recognize it themselves or articulate it better to another? Therefore, if I asked someone, "How are you feeling," I'd like to know the intensity of that feeling or emotion, since I'd likely respond differently based upon their response.

During my workshops on emotional literacy, I ask the attendees to break into small groups of three or four. Then I ask them to take turns within the group to come up with as many words as they can to further describe an emotion and its different intensities. At the end of that exercise, to see how many specific words the group came up with, we go around the room. Here are some examples from high intensity to medium to low: Happy—elated, ecstatic, excited to satisfied and gratified to glad and contented. Angry—enraged, livid, and irate to mad, frustrated, and pissed to annoyed and upset. Sad—depressed and miserable to melancholy to disappointed. Fear—terrified and petrified to apprehensive and intimidated to worried and nervous/anxious. Shame—remorseful and disgraced to guilty and embarrassed to regretful. There were many aha, light-bulb moments for the students as they thought about all the different words that can be used to more specifically and accurately describe what they are feeling, If you were in my workshop that day, what other words would you have come up with for each emotion?

To enhance one's emotional literacy further, Six Seconds recommends the following in their development report:[7] Learn from people you believe to be emotionally literate and ask them what they are feeling and the intensity of that feeling at any moment. To gain even better insight, ask them to identify and understand where that emotion is coming from. Journal a list of words that best describe what you might feel at different times of the day and expand that vocabulary over the course of time. I've done so since learning more about words that most accurately describe an emotion and have my go-tos. As an example, I was at a large meeting one evening that became very contentious, almost to fisticuffs, when it should not have been (I was not directly involved in the fracas). When I came home my wife noticed I was angry and called me out on it. However, I wasn't "just angry," I was distraught, disheartened, disgusted, dejected, discouraged, and finally, plain disappointed. I had my specific go-to words that were much more descriptive and accurate that made it easier for my wife to understand that I wasn't "just" angry. Of course, true to Six Seconds's suggestions, she next wanted to know what generated these emotions, i.e., what happened. I gave her the play-by-play.

At the end of my workshops, I ask the attendees a trick question: "Which emotions are good, and which are bad?" Happily, they catch the trick quickly and recognize that emotions aren't good or bad; they are just information that you can use or ignore, though to ignore the value of the information that emotions are offering is perilous, like ignoring a patient's history, physical examination, lab, imaging, or cardiac results. Your emotions are trying to tell you something too. The question is, "Are you listening?"

One of the other great values of being aware of your emotions is that they tend to show up in your body language or in your facial expressions, unless you are a very good poker player. Like many, I am not, and that's why for most of us, even if we aren't saying it, our emotions show up on our faces and in our body language. As an example, a student of mine once told me that people thought she had an RBF. "What is an RBF?" I asked naively. She answered, "Resting Bitch Face." I asked her what she was thinking and feeling when someone said that to her, and she replied that she was skeptical, even cynical, not trusting what the person was saying. What was in her mind showed on her face.

Virtual meeting platforms have been a wonderful advancement in many ways (likely the only good thing to come out of the COVID pandemic), including giving feedback as to what others were seeing based upon what one was feeling and thinking. On one Zoom call a physician friend mentioned to me that I looked very grouchy. And he was right. I was grouchy. From then on, in addition to noticing how others were looking on Zoom, I'd also look at myself, especially if I was thinking something negative, skeptical, or untrusting.

As we gradually came out of the COVID epidemic and returned to in-person meetings, I became more alert and would catch myself thinking about something that was being said at the meeting and then recognizing that it was showing up on my face. On harried days in the office, feeling rushed and overly stressed, I recall patients asking me if I was okay, clearly reading my facial expressions and body language. Maybe they were worried about me, though maybe they were even more worried about themselves, since if I wasn't okay then maybe the treatments I was offering them wouldn't be okay.

While we clinicians or nurses are doing the "eyeball test," when we walk into the exam or hospital room assessing if the patient is sick or not, the patient is doing their own eyeball test, looking at us and assessing our facial expressions and body language. Their thoughts: Are they safe or not? Do they trust us or not? What do you think our patients might think if we walked into the room looking calm versus harried? Sure versus unsure? Caring versus uncaring? Energized versus exhausted?

I experienced the patient side when my oldest granddaughter, the dancer, had an ankle fracture. I went with her and my daughter to the pediatric orthopedic surgeon's appointment. The surgeon whirled into the room, looking very rushed and harried, likely reflecting that he had many patients waiting for him that day and trying to stay on schedule. He stopped to shake our hands, though in so doing he didn't pause to look us in the eye but rather was looking toward his desk and the computer. Needless to say, the rest of the appointment didn't go well. My daughter and I had many questions and with each one we could easily see, based upon the facial expression and body language, that the surgeon's patience was waning as his internal clock was ticking. We left the appointment not feeling seen, heard, or appreciated and with many questions unanswered. Though we didn't question the surgeon's competence or recommendations, based upon his bedside manner we had concerns about his level of caring and investment in my granddaughter's case. What did we do? What most dissatisfied patients would do. We pursued a second opinion and went to another pediatric orthopedic surgeon. Coincidentally, they spent the same amount of time with us as the former physician and agreed with the medical management. However, based upon their social interactions—sitting, making eye contact with us instead of with the computer, generously listening, relaxed and being fully present from beginning to end, patiently answering all of our questions—we came away feeling heard and confident with their recommendations. Bottom line: what's in your mind shows up in your body and on your face, and being self-aware of that can make the difference between a patient staying with you or not.

The value of being able to identify, recognize, and understand our emotions and their intensity is that we can better deal with them when they are less intense—a pimple as opposed to an abscess. Emotions can fester and intensify, especially if we try to suppress them. If we are unable to label our emotions, we will be less likely to make good decisions, be more likely to have a narrow zone, or worse, be bumped out, since, as will be discussed in Chapter 9, the best decisions are made with part logic and part emotion.

Combining the "Check-in" with Emotional Literacy

Now that you have read through the self-awareness, check-in, and emotional literacy sections and are well schooled on the zone concept, let's practice using them all and determine what emotion(s) is/are evoked, what the intensity of the emotion(s) is/are, and what is the wideness, or not, of your zone as you picture checking in with each of the following scenarios:

- You're a student, and a preceptor is angry about something you did or didn't do, and lets you know about it in front of your peers.

- A longtime patient of yours who you cared for deeply has just passed away.

- A pediatric patient of yours has just been cured of their cancer, thanks to your good work.

- A patient or a friend of yours begins to cry—and you have time. What if you were pinched for time?

- You just had an oops moment in the OR or while doing a procedure in the cath or GI lab or in the emergency department.

- Your study partner did much better on the exam than you did.

- A patient's family is furious because you didn't call them back.

- You're a nurse and your patient is mad at you because you didn't answer their call bell fast enough.

- Your patient said "thank you" for your good care.

How did you do with your check-in? Were you able to identify the width of your zone? How long did it take you to do so? If you said, "in a heartbeat," that would be typical. Our limbic system, our emotional brain, is very responsive. Were you able to feel that emotion and its intensity? As I hope you can appreciate, emotional literacy is an important element of being self-aware; recognizing patterns is another.

Recognizing Patterns Is Good Medicine and High EQ

Recognizing patterns is fundamental and foundational to being emotionally intelligent while helping us stay in our zone and keeping it wide. It's a fabulous skill, summarized by the philosopher George Santayana, who wrote, "Those who cannot remember the past are condemned to repeat it."[8] By recognizing your patterns, knowing, understanding, and anticipating what is coming, you can be proactive and prepared versus reactive and unprepared for a challenging situation, especially one that you have experienced before. The adage attributed to Ben Franklin says it best: "Failing to prepare is preparing to fail."

As a clinician or nurse, recognizing patterns is how we make diagnoses. We listen to a patient's history, note a series of signs and symptoms, add a physical exam, some labs and imaging tests, then put all information together, recognize the pattern, and make a diagnosis. Consider this example in my field of endocrinology. A person with a family history of autoimmune diseases is complaining of fatigue, unintentional weight gain, feeling cold even during the heat of the summer, loss of hair, and deepening of their voice. You find they have a slow heart rate, high blood pressure, are mildly hypothermic, have coarse hair and cold skin, loss of the lateral aspect of their eyebrows, no palpable thyroid gland, a voice that sounds frog-like, and they are wearing heavy wool socks and a beanie hat on an eighty-degree summer day. Add in lab tests: high cholesterol and calcium levels, low serum sodium, and enlarged red blood cells (macrocytosis). Based upon this pattern of signs and symptoms, the physical exam, and laboratory findings, you suspect hypothyroidism and order thyroid function tests, which come back with another pattern, an elevated TSH (thyroid-stimulating hormone) and a low free T4 level, consistent with primary hypothyroidism, most likely due to Hashimoto's disease.

As a nurse, you might recognize a pattern with how you respond to patients with certain diagnoses like psychiatric illnesses, non-compliant patients who are frequently readmitted to the hospital or keep coming back to the office, or unmotivated patients who don't put effort or energy into getting better.

As a student, you might notice patterns when you are taking repeated multiple-choice tests and get good at passing the tests with the same professor. You get a feel for the kinds of questions they ask and the choice of answers that they give. We found in our research that students' abilities to recognize patterns was one of the EQ competencies that increased during their academic, first year, the didactic year, possibly associated with taking endless multiple-choice exams. Their consequential thinking also increased, probably associated with studying so many facts, using logic, and being tested. This improvement in their abilities to recognize patterns and consequential logical thinking may be considered examples of neuroplasticity (chapter 3) and reinforce that EQ is learnable and a competency.

Recognizing patterns can make or break an interaction with a patient or their family. Recalling what went well or didn't go well in previous conversations with other patients and families—including what you said, how you said it, what your facial and body language conveyed, along with picking up on the other person's verbal and nonverbal signals—can help you when you are in conversation with the current patient or family member. While replicating what worked is valuable, avoiding or adjusting to what didn't work is also very valuable so you don't repeat the same mistakes.

An example that I described in an earlier chapter, where I was not my best self to a patient's grandson who was inquiring about his grandmother's anemia, was a "learn the hard way" moment never to repeat. I subsequently recognized the situation/pattern and when I came across another person who was questioning me about a medical situation, I immediately became self-aware, recognized the pattern, and recalled that earlier conversation so as not to repeat the mistake I made in the past. If the situation occurred when my zone was narrow or I was bumped out of my zone, I would try grounding myself and if I couldn't, I would ask if it would be okay if I got back to them later.

One of the coachees I was working with used the recognize-pattern concept to a tee. He described being out to dinner with a couple of his partners, one of whom was a known instigator, a provocateur, who frequently got under my coachee's skin, provoking friction. While at dinner that night, the provocateur again started to instigate and irritate my coachee. This time, however, instead of being in autopilot and falling into the same trap of allowing himself to get sucked in, amped up and agitated, which would inflame the interaction, he checked in with himself, hit the pause button, recognized his past nonproductive pattern, excused himself, went to the bathroom to regroup and widen his zone, then came back, calmer, ready to deal with the hijinks coming his way.

There are many examples of patterns worth recognizing so you can prepare for them in advance, assuming you can't avoid them—like the patients on your schedule that day that you need to see—and help keep you in your zone. These include interacting with people who test your patience and tolerance, like long talkers, especially when you are short on time, or those who hold information back, are always complaining and are never satisfied, or who don't follow your recommendations. It's good to know how you interacted with them in the past, knowing what worked and didn't, rather than allowing them to bump you out of your zone with each interaction.

Recognizing patterns is not just important to you professionally. It is also extremely important in that it can impact a person's ability to survive, even subconsciously. I suspect we've all been driving on a highway behind a truck in the right lane and wanted to pass it, only to recognize the pattern of another vehicle coming up quickly in the left-hand lane. Recognizing that pattern helps us be patient and allow that fast-moving vehicle to pass us, then allowing us to safely pass the truck. You can probably think of many more patterns in life that help you survive and thrive.

Sometimes we might not be anticipating a situation but then it arises in real time. It is advantageous to recognize that we've been in a similar situation in the past. Consider the hidden reasons why patients come to see you, their clinician. Before you know it, and unanticipated, the conversation shifts dramatically to the fact that they are really upset with you about a mistake they thought you made, something you said at the last visit, not calling them back quickly enough, or a staff person who upset them. It feels like the patients always do this at the *end* of the office visit when you are ready to move on to your next patient. Then the patient says, "Doc, there's one more thing . . ." That's when your zone narrows, especially if you are behind in your office schedule for the day. You start to feel anxious, nervous, irritated, or agitated. At that time it's good to remind yourself that you've been in these situations before, recognizing the pattern, and recall what worked and didn't work and respond accordingly.

Need another example of the benefit of recognizing patterns? As a member of our academic support team, called Magis (Magis means more in Latin), I work with students who are struggling to pass their classes. They come to our Magis meetings often feeling defeated, fearing that they are going to fail out of our program. I then ask them if they have been in similar stressful situations before, whether associated with school or sports, i.e., doubting their ability to be successful. Invariably, the answer is yes. I ask them to consider that pattern and what they did that allowed them to be resilient and succeed. As they describe their strategies, I can easily see their confidence growing.

How does one become better at recognizing patterns? According to Six Seconds,[9] one strategy is to use this simple formula:

When (stimulus), I (response).

Examples can be when I am: stressed, anxious, sad, happy, or afraid, I . . . (insert response). Or every time you interact with a particular personality you . . . or every time this particular patient comes into the office you . . . or every time you have more to do than time or energy allows you . . . or every time someone gives you a gift or compliment you . . .

I bring up this last example because I struggled with it for years. This came to a head when I was out to dinner with a group of friends and one of my former residents came over to the table and generously told me how much she appreciated all that I taught her during her training. Feeling a little embarrassed, I downplayed the compliment, saying, "I must have had a good day back then." I could see that comment didn't land well with her and frankly it didn't feel good to me either. The next day, as I replayed that scenario, I recalled an advice article from Ann Landers from years prior. She wrote that if someone gives you a compliment, the best thing to say is "thank you." So simple. With that I called up my former resident, apologized for my flippant response, then told her how much I appreciated her gratitude and said, "thank you."

Journaling how you thought, felt, and responded to certain situations at the end of the day or week can also be very valuable. Then reviewing what you wrote, looking for themes and patterns, can also be very helpful for identifying your responses to similar stimuli. Another method, which does take a little courage and bravery, is to ask someone you respect and trust to give you feedback on what they see you do and say. Hopefully you would receive the information as useful, productive, and constructive feedback and are grateful rather than defensive. Note that if you do receive feedback, you have the option and control of accepting the comments, rejecting them, or considering their value.

The result of these strategies to enhance your self-awareness is that you are more likely to be in your zone and to keep your zone wide. You'll be less likely to be bumped out when the going gets tough, and it always gets tough when dealing with people who are ill, the health-care system, the intensity of health-care education, and life in general.

Putting EQ into Action

Read the following scenario and ask yourself the following: *Before entering this patient's room and interacting with the patient and the family, and knowing what is coming, I need to check in with myself. What is the width of my zone? What specific emotions is this situation evoking? What is the intensity of those emotions?*

You're a clinician, nurse, or student on your clinical rotation giving ongoing care for a patient in the hospital who has advanced illnesses, in the setting of advanced dementia. Medically, you see little to no hope that the patient will make any significant recovery. Even if they did, they would return to a full-care status and, as you see it, a very low quality of life, unable to communicate meaningfully, nor feed or toilet themselves. Despite this, the family, who are the decision makers, are pushing you to do everything you can to "save" the patient, even if it means pursuing aggressive interventions including full resuscitation. You are concerned you are not maintaining your Hippocratic Oath of practicing medicine or nursing: "first, do no harm, *primum non nocere*."

Chapter Takeaways

1. Self-awareness helps us understand our thoughts, feelings, actions, patterns, and if we are in our zone or not (internal self-awareness). It also helps us know how we are perceived by others (external self-awareness). While it is foundational and fundamental to emotional intelligence, the competency is not very common. However, like all components of emotional intelligence, it is learnable.

2. The check-in, which only takes a moment, gives us the opportunity to know how we are thinking and feeling and if we are in our zones or not. This can be of great value when it comes to knowing what we do or say next.

3. Emotions are not good or bad; rather, they are information. They are trying to tell us something. Ignore them at our own peril. Being emotionally literate helps us be very specific identifying and describing our emotions, their intensity, where they might be coming from, and what they are trying to tell us.

4. Emotions tend to show up as facial expressions and body language. If it's not coming out of our mouths, it may still show up on our faces for all to see and assess.

5. Recognizing patterns, even if they sneak up on you, can be a wonderful asset to better managing your day by recalling past situations, in your personal and professional lives, that worked and didn't work. Doing this takes you off autopilot and helps avoid repeating past errors that might have brought you regrets or remorse.

6. We can improve upon our ability to recognize our patterns by journaling, asking someone we trust for their insights or using the simple formula: When (stimulus), I (response).

Chapter 8

Social Awareness

The eyes have one language everywhere.

—GEORGE HERBERT

Not long before writing this book, I met a friend's father who had just lost his wife of over fifty years. I could easily see that his zone was very narrow, and he was feeling despondent and distraught, based upon his facial expression (lowered corners of his mouth, eyelids and eyebrows down), body language (lowered head, slumped shoulders, moving slowly), and his voice (lower pitch, slower speed, lack of energy). Heck, I've seen and heard those signs many times before in others. Recognizing those cues, I responded to his loss with sincerity.

"Oh my," I said, "that is so heartbreaking. I can see how much you loved your wife and are missing her terribly. What a huge loss. How are you holding up?"

He immediately knew that I "felt him." In a heartbeat we connected. Sometime later I again saw my friend and asked her how her father was doing. She said he continues to feel profound sadness from his loss though he still talks favorably about that brief conversation I had with him. It's amazing how showing someone you genuinely care can be so meaningful and a good lesson for clinicians and nurses in a busy practice who have limited time with each patient. It doesn't take long to connect if you can pick up on someone's cues by being socially aware.

The truth is that when I suffered from significant losses in my past, I felt exactly how my friend's father felt: distraught, distressed, depressed. The point is that people who are self-aware may also be better at being socially aware. Bradberry and Greaves define social awareness as "the ability to identify, recognize, and understand the emotions in other people and to know what they are thinking and feeling."[1] It's easier to do so if you can recognize that you have felt the same, even if it wasn't the exact same situation. Additionally, we've all felt different intensities of anger, fear, shame, and happiness. We can use these feelings to connect with how someone else is feeling, which is just the beginning.

The benefit of being socially aware is that once you know how you are thinking and feeling and can pick up on another's cues about how they are doing, it helps with the next step, which is what do you do and say (self-management), and how does what you do and say impact your relationship (relationship-management).

Additionally, being socially aware helps you with timing and when to interact with someone, the proverbial "reading the room." Or consider the adage "timing is everything." Say or do the right thing at the wrong time and it usually doesn't work in your favor, worsening a situation or a relationship. I offer the following examples to the attendees in my workshops, asking them to raise their hands if the timing is right: suggesting to a patient who is going through a rough patch in life to quit smoking; asking a surgeon in the middle of a very stressful, chaotic oops moment in the OR what are other potential complications of the procedure; asking another nurse who is harried, obviously overwhelmed in the middle of juggling multiple complicated patients, to watch your own patients while you are taking a break; confronting another student who spread a nasty rumor about you while they are out at a restaurant enjoying themselves with another group of students. I'm happy to report that, given these examples, no one raised their hand for any of these obvious situations though they appreciated the intent and spirit of the exercise. Now that you know what social awareness is and the enormous value of it, the next piece is how to get better at it. Read on.

Are They in Their EQ Zone? How Do You Know?

The first step to being socially aware is to identify, recognize, and understand people's facial expressions, body language, and voice pattern. It's knowing that 93 percent of communication is not with the spoken word, otherwise known as Mehrabian's Rule.[2] Picking up on these cues requires listening to learn from the tone, timbre, pitch, and volume of the voice. Sometimes it's not *what* is being said but rather *how* it is said. Consider a common phrase, "why did you do that?" One way to phrase it is in an indignant, judging way. Another is with interest and curiosity. Additionally, as Susan Scott points out in her book *Fierce Conversations*, it's also worthwhile when listening to the actual words for *content* (what are they telling you), *intent* (why are they telling you this), and *emotions* (what they are feeling as they are telling you something).[3] To summarize this section and to quote myself, with a nod to Yogi Berra, "You can hear a lot just by listening." And to help introduce you to the next section, Yogi actually said, "You can see a lot just by looking," which leads me to the topic of listening with your eyes.

It helps to listen to another with your eyes, picking up on facial expressions and body language. The great thing about body language and facial expressions is that they tend to be universal and cross cultures.

People from different cultures share about 70 percent of the facial expressions used in response to different social and emotional situations. This supports Darwin's theory that expressing emotion in our faces is universal among humans.[4]

Consider what you will see, probably any place in the world, when someone is out of their zone and angry: a flushed face, furrowed eyebrows, tense lips, a protruding or clenched jaw, and even more intensely, bared teeth, flailing arms, and a protruding chest. How about in a narrow zone when someone is embarrassed: covering their face with their hands, blushing, avoiding eye contact, a nervous smile, lowered head, fidgeting, looking away from others, and a shrinking appearance trying to minimize attention. In a wide zone and happy: a genuine smile with raised cheeks and crinkled eyes, an upright posture, relaxed body movements, open body language like uncrossed arms, good eye contact, and even animated gestures like nodding or clapping.

Patients will also recognize your body language in that sitting means much more than standing (standing might also connote you having power over them). Having your feet pointed toward them if you were standing also connotes a different message versus feet pointing away from them. Maybe the most obvious body language message is when clinicians or nurses stand with their hand on the doorknob as they are talking with their patient, which is saying "the appointment is over, and I am leaving." Recognizing the value and importance of body language in relationship building and maintenance, a personal example would be if I am watching TV and my wife wants to tell me something, I'll mute the TV and turn and face her, letting her know that she has my full attention, I am present. Here. Now.

These examples may seem obvious if you are already socially aware and using the skills of listening with your ears and eyes, though they might serve as reminders to pick up on these cues when you might not be your best self and in your own zone. One word of caution is this:

If the physical cues are not consistent with the verbal cues, then that might be a red flag as to the reliability of what you or the other person is communicating.

A second step to being socially aware is not as overt as the timing nor as obvious as facial expressions, body language, and voice. It's recognizing that not everybody thinks and acts like you do. Six Seconds has, as part of its SEI assessment, a Brain Profile that quantifies how people *focus*, *make decisions*, and what *drives* them.[5] People tend to *focus* on being either rational/analytical on one extreme and emotional on the other extreme. As an example, when one walks into a room, the analytical person might focus on the number of chairs or people present while the emotional person might focus on how it feels to be in that place; what's the vibe. Personally, I am more on the emotional side of the continuum in that situation, such that when I walk into a room, a store, or a hospital, the first thing I sense is whether or not it feels good to be there, comfortable, and safe. When it comes to *decision*-making, some might be risk adverse (evaluative), while others might be risk takers (innovative). Lastly, what *drives* some is being practical and getting the job done today, while others are idealistic, visionary, thinking about the future.

The great value of the brain preference is twofold. First, it's being self-aware and recognizing what your brain preferences are and how you focus, how you make decisions, and what drives you. In practicality, if you are not taking actions in alignment with your brain preferences, they may not be the correct actions for you. The second value of brain preferences is social awareness, helping you clue into what others focus on, how they make decisions, and what drives them. Knowing this can be helpful especially when explaining a diagnosis and treatment plan to patients.

Take a person with new-onset type 1, autoimmune, diabetes mellitus, requiring insulin. Now, imagine you were explaining the diagnosis and treatment plan to an engineer who has a scientist brain preference, someone who stereotypically *focuses* on being detailed, accurate, careful, and precise, especially with things they can measure, who is risk-averse and ultra-careful in their *decision*-making and *driven* by practicalities, like what they need to get through today. You might initially discuss the details and facts of monitoring their blood glucoses and administering insulin, including when to take it, where to inject it, and the doses needed based upon carb counting. On the other end of the spectrum, if you were explaining new-onset type 1 diabetes to someone who has a "visionary" brain preference, perhaps an artist, who is more focused on emotions than details, a risk taker, and driven by how this diagnosis is going to affect their future, you might initially say that if one had to have type 1 diabetes, this is the best year to have it, since every year the treatments are better and people can live relatively well, long-term. In short, being socially aware and astute in recognizing the brain preferences of the person you are interacting with can be an advantage when it comes to self and relationship management.

Other benefits of understanding your brain preference and those of others are worth highlighting. The first involves being in a leadership position and responsible for hiring your team. If you hire people who have the same brain preferences that you do—the proverbial "bobble-heads" and "yes-people"—you might feel good and secure: "They are a good fit because they think like me." However, your team might have deficits in identifying and fixing problems or being critical of a new idea, not seeing it from all the different perspectives that may come from a room filled with people who have different brain preferences.

Another value of recognizing others' brain preferences is being socially aware of who you might seek out for advice for a particular problem or concern you are having. As a clinician or nurse, there might be times when you need help with a technical issue, something that requires a calculation of a dose of medication or how to maximize your use of the electronic medical record or use a device in a procedure lab or in the operating room. Other times you might need advice related to a more social/emotional issue, like how to deal with a challenging patient, colleague, or direct report who made a hard day harder for you. I suspect you might not want to seek advice from someone whose brain preference is more on the emotional side for your technical problem and someone who is technical for your social/emotional concerns. Knowing the brain preferences of the people in your network and community can go a long way toward getting you the advice you need when you need it and not causing the person you are seeking assistance from to feel badly because they couldn't and/or didn't have the skill set to help you with your issue.

Two other quick benefits of understanding another person's brain preference have to do with negotiating a deal and sharing an idea. If you are negotiating something with someone, knowing how they focus, how they make decisions, and what drives them can be an asset for you; you will be better prepared to offer your points in a way they can digest, and increase your chances of getting what you want. Additionally, asking an analytical thinker about an emotionally charged idea might not be met with an opinion that is meaningful for you, and vice versa for asking an emotional-leaning person to give you an opinion on something very analytical.

If you want to learn/quantify what your brain preference is, even if you may have an idea already, and maybe even gain greater understanding of the brain preference of others, you can complete the Six Seconds's SEI assessment.[6] (Contact Six Seconds at www.6seconds.org.) Additionally, from completing that survey, one can take an even deeper dive and learn more about their brain talents, which gives even greater insights into how you think.[7] Do you **focus** on data mining and prioritizing or connection and collaboration? When you make **decisions**, are you a critical thinker and adaptable or are you more imaginative and risk resilient? What talents **drive** you? Commitment and problem-solving or being visionary? If you are making decisions that are not in alignment with your talents, maybe those decisions aren't the best ones for you.

How to Be (Even) More Socially Aware

How can one become better at being socially aware? Six Seconds recommends the following:[8] (1) Sit on a bench in a crowded park or fair or mall and people-watch, preferably with someone who is very socially aware. Watch a passerby's body language and facial expressions and make up a story about their scenario and what they are feeling and thinking. (2) Watch a silent movie and try to label the emotions that the characters are feeling throughout the picture show. In my workshops I like to show a Charlie Chaplin scene from 1928 entitled "The Lion Cage." The clip is about three minutes long. I then ask the attendees to name all the different emotions that they observed during the clip and describe the facial expressions and body language that helped them to conclude what emotions they saw. There were many, including fear, surprise, sadness, and joy. I also like to show static pictures of people with different facial expressions and body languages that reflect different emotions and see how good the attendees are at identifying those emotions. (Overall, very good.) Of note, I encourage the attendees to focus on the eyes first. They are the "window" to see through what one is really thinking and feeling.

As I conclude this chapter, I am listening with my mind's eye, picturing you reading it and hoping that your body language and facial expressions are emitting cues suggesting some joy, enlightenment, and reflection. I am also picturing listening with my ears to a conversation you might be having with another, describing the contents of this chapter with a tone, pitch, timbre, and volume of voice that is indicating excitement, enthusiasm, and eagerness. I see you relaying your takeaways from the chapter to the right people in the right place at the right time, since timing is everything. I am hoping that you are offering your takeaways to others, recognizing their specific brain preferences—telling the analytical person some specific details from the book, and telling the person who tends to focus more emotionally about how the book can help you and them connect even more deeply. If you are doing all this, then both you and I are leaving this chapter more socially aware than when we began. Now that we are more so, it's time to take a deeper dive into what we do and say, now that we recognize how we think and feel with greater insights into our self- and social awareness.

Putting EQ into Action

Read the following scenarios and ask yourself the following: *How might I use social awareness to identify, recognize, and understand what the other person is thinking and feeling? When is the right time to address the issue? How might understanding the other person's brain preferences be valuable when it's time to interact?*

1. You're a clinician caring for another clinician whom you just diagnosed with cirrhosis. When you walk into the room, you see them sitting nervously, fidgeting on the exam table, waiting to hear about their new diagnosis and what to do about it.

2. You're a nurse, and when you walk into the exam room you see a patient sitting on the exam table who looks disheveled, with clothes tattered, hair uncombed, face unshaven, and head down. When you introduce yourself, they don't look up or make eye contact. They look like they've been crying.

3. You're a student on your clinical rotation with a burning question about the pathophysiology of a disease you are studying, which you want to ask your preceptor. They come out of an exam room looking very harried, rushed, and distracted.

Chapter Takeaways

1. Social awareness is the ability to pick up verbal, and even more important, nonverbal cues from another to know if they are in their zone or not. It's the ability to read the room and a competency that you can improve upon with practice and desire.

2. Knowing if someone is in their zone or not can influence the timing and type of interaction you might have with them.

3. There is great value in knowing your brain preference and the brain preference of the person you are interacting with, since it can help guide your interaction and relationship with them.

Chapter 9

Self-Management

Life is 10 percent what happens to me
and 90 percent how I react to it.

—CHARLES SWINDOLL

I t's been said that the average person makes more than 35,000 decisions each day. As I reflect on my days in private practice, I think I used my 35,000 just on making decisions for the twenty-plus patients I saw each day. Each patient had multiple medical conditions that needed to be addressed with each visit: hypertension, diabetes and its complications, hyperlipidemia, cardiovascular disease, osteoporosis, thyroid disease, and depression, to name a few. For each decision I had to ask myself, What are the choices I have to manage this condition, not to mention what will the patient be willing to do? Take more medicine? Less medicine? Nutritional or activity modifications? More testing? No changes at all? And that is the gist of self-management. It's all about understanding and recognizing the choices we have and being intentional with the decisions that we make.

Stephen Covey, author of *The 7 Habits of Highly Effective People*, stated, "I am not a product of my circumstances. I am a product of my decisions."[1] Author Graham Brown summarizes the significance of decision-making best with this quote: "Life is about choices. Some we regret, some we're proud of. Some will haunt us forever. The message: we are what we chose to be."[2] Think about all the choices you had and the decisions you had to make to get you where you are today in your professional career: the decision to study hard and make sacrifices, the decision to apply to schools, and the decision to choose a school and a profession. You get the picture. The question is, how do we make the best decisions possible for ourselves to help us get what we want and want to avoid? The answer begins with self- and social awareness.

Once you know how you think and feel, whether you are in your zone or not, then recognizing what others think and feel, and whether they are in their zone or not, the next step is managing yourself by recognizing your choices and then making decisions. According to Bradberry and Greaves, the definition of self-management is "the ability to use your awareness of your emotions to stay flexible and direct your behavior positively . . . [and manage] your emotional reactions to situations and people."[3]

Self-management is deciding how you act, what you say, and how you say it. It's how you show up to others. People will only see what you say and do. They will not see, or necessarily care about, what was going on inside you and whether you were in your zone or not. Rather, for you, knowing what is below the surface, and specifically what you are thinking and feeling and if you are in your zone or not, will go a long way toward helping you make your best decisions.

In one exercise I do in my workshops to help attendees better understand the choices that they have and then be intentional with their decisions, I offer them a series of scenarios and have them contrast good decisions with less good ones, i.e., what do they do or say in each scenario. Articulating the less good decisions may make it easier for the attendees to recognize better decisions. Using examples that are appropriate for the PA students, I offer them these situations (note that the less good management responses conjure up a lot of fun and laughter as well as insights):

- You've been studying hard, now it's late and you are not retaining anything. The test is in the morning.
- You're stuck on a few questions during your test.
- Someone in the class said something negative about you and you found out.
- You disagreed with a professor about a test question answer.
- Someone cut you off while you were driving.

The same type of exercise can be used for clinicians and nurses, of course, with different more relatable scenarios such as: you're ravishingly hangry before seeing your next patient, or a patient asks you a question that you really don't know the answer to, or the chief medical or nursing officer calls you into their office to discuss a negative interaction you had with a colleague, or a patient says something micro aggressive to you or comes on to you. What do you do or say in each situation that would be good self-management vs. less good? You have a choice. It's important to remember, though, that just because someone made a less good decision doesn't mean they are a bad or weak person, as one of my students commented. They just made a less good decision at that moment (which we all have done). Ideally, we can all understand where that less good decision came from, learn from them, and not repeat them.

Self-management and the decisions that one makes can also impact their reputation. I always ask the students who attend my workshops to raise their hands if they would like a good reputation. Invariably, every hand goes up. I suspect if I asked a group of clinicians and nurses to raise their hands whether they wanted a good reputation, all the hands would also go up. I then offer the students scenarios that can make or break their reputation depending on the decisions that they make, i.e., what they do and say. Here is a short list of situations I offer them:

- You didn't do as well on your test as you wanted. You feel disgusted and like a failure.

- You said something hurtful to someone, and it got back to them. You feel guilty and embarrassed.

- You suffered the loss of a close relationship. You feel heartbroken and melancholy.

Scenarios that might be more relevant to clinicians and nurses might be how they interacted with a colleague with whom they had a disagreement, or how they managed themselves when they felt stressed having more patients to see than time or energy allowed, or how they communicated a diagnosis and treatment plan especially to a patient with low health literacy. It's all about knowing your choices and making decisions in alignment with what you want. In this case, a good reputation. The next question is how do you make your best decisions? Read on.

How to Make Your Best Decisions

One morning I came downstairs after a restless night's sleep and feeling like I hadn't slept at all, and declared to my wife, "I am going to make a significant change in my work." She looked at me, easily noticed my very tired-looking face, shook her head, and gently replied, "This is not the right time to make a quick decision. Why don't you pause, take your time, until you are not exhausted and sleep deprived. You are not your best self right now" (interpretation, you are not in your zone). She was right . . . again.

Another exercise I offer the students to make the point about the timing of decision-making is to, again, give them scenarios and ask them to raise their hands if the timing is right to make a good decision. Here are examples of what I give them:

- You're totally focused, concentrating hard for long hours, studying for your finals.

- You're angry about something.

- You're feeling sad, somber, even depressed.

- You're in a good frame of mind, feeling content and satisfied.

Most of the hands go up for the final scenario. I suspect many if not most clinicians and nurses might relate to these scenarios and agree. The timing of the decision, whether you're in your zone or not, could be the difference between making a good one and less good one.

Some decisions can be made quickly, while others may best be made slowly. Daniel Kahneman described quick versus slow, more deliberate thinking in his book *Thinking, Fast and Slow*.[4] The key is to recognize which decisions we can make quickly and which ones need more time because they need more thought and consideration. Consider the patient with new-onset hypertension, spontaneous hypokalemia, and metabolic alkalosis. Is it Cushing's? Pheochromocytoma? Renal artery stenosis? Or primary hyperaldosteronism? You might want to take more time to think through this one to make the correct diagnosis versus less time needed to make the diagnosis in someone with a diffuse rash after using a new soap or laundry detergent. BTW, the former scenario is primary hyperaldosteronism.

Jonah Lehrer, in his book *How We Decide*, says that the best decisions are made when one combines logic and emotions.[5] This might sound antithetical to people who were told growing up to be logical and rational when making decisions and "don't be so emotional." Unfortunately, according to Lehrer, that is a mistake. The wise person uses both emotion and logic, and doing so can make your decision-making more efficient and effective.

I was using both logic and emotion in my clinical decision-making even before I realized I was doing it. I would go through a complicated patient history, do a physical exam, assess all the lab, cardiac, and imaging data, and then make my diagnosis. However, just when I thought I had the final answer and the case buttoned up, there was "something" telling me that something wasn't right. That "something" was a feeling, a gnawing type of sensation in my gut. I then had a choice. I could ignore that feeling or I could recognize it and use it as information. I learned early on that "that something" was a great friend and saved me, and my patient, from me missing something critical in their case. That feeling made me reassess the details of the case and find "that something" that I was missing or overlooked. When I did, that feeling dissipated. Had I just used logic I could/would have missed that detail.

The additional problem with just using logic is that it can get you stuck in your decision-making, having you go back and forth between the pros and cons, benefits, and costs of the decision, not feeling which is the best choice to make. Before I began using emotion with logic, for example, I could sometimes feel myself getting stuck when trying to decide on a dose of Augmentin—500 or 875 mg—for a patient's sinusitis or bronchitis. Conversely, using all emotion in your decision-making can make you susceptible to impulsive behaviors, e.g., without thinking it through, prescribe the Augmentin without checking to see if the patient has a penicillin allergy.

To make the point about using both logic and emotions to make the best decision, an NP asked me for a curbside consult on how to adjust a dose of insulin on a patient with hyperglycemia and diabetes. She gave me a quick review of the case. I *logically* contemplated all the variables such as the patient's renal and liver disease, the fact that they were on steroids, were emotionally stressed, weren't eating, and had an infection on top of it all. I began to suggest a dose of insulin to lower the glucose. However, as I began to say it, I "felt" a quick unsettledness that the dose I was about to suggest was too aggressive and could overshoot, causing hypoglycemia. In short, my logical suggestion just didn't feel right and potentially could have broken one of my rules of "what I want" (safe patient care) and "what I don't want" (a medical complication). Once I added the information of what *felt* like the right, safe dose, a dose that would give benefit without risking a negative side effect, my decision-making became easier.

Some life choices, especially the real big ones, do require additional deliberation. One of the exercises that Six Seconds recommends in their SEI development report is called "Emotional Algebra."[6] It can be especially valuable for those who like to make pros-and-cons lists. For example, you are thinking about joining a medical practice. You list the pros: good pay, good clinicians to work with, good organizational culture and climate. The cons: it's in a location that is not desirable to you and your family, the cost of living is high, the schools are relatively weak. With emotional algebra, in addition to listing the pros and cons, you assign an emotional impact number of 1 through 10, with 10 being the greatest emotional impact and 1 being the least. Now let's go through the list again. Pros: Good pay: 8. Good clinicians to work with: 8. Good organizational culture and climate: 7. The cons: It's in a location that is not desirous to you and your family: 10. The cost of living is high: 8. The schools are relatively weak: 9. When you total up the columns, the emotional impact of the pros is 23. The cons total 27. Conclusion? Maybe taking that job is not the best decision for you and your family.

In addition to using logic and emotions to make the best decisions to keep you in your zone and keep it wide, add intrinsic motivation.

Intrinsic motivation is what you are truly committed to and value. It's the antithesis of extrinsic motivation, which is deciding to do something for reasons that will get you something like fame, fortune, power, or money, or alternatively for fear or punishment that may put you in a position to be a victim or a hostage to that desire (e.g., a golden handcuff). Making decisions that are in alignment with what you truly value often leads to greater fulfillment.

During my workshops, I ask attendees to list what truly intrinsically motivates them. Here is what they say: Harmony. Peace. Collaboration. Relationships. Kindness. Trust. Caring. Compassion. Consistency. Competency. Commitment. Accomplishments. Honesty/Integrity. Fairness. Equality. Community. Hard work. Being productive. Reaching their goals. If they are making decisions that are not in alignment with what intrinsically motivates them, maybe it is not their best decision. What would be on your list?

I was once working with a group of fourth-year OB-GYN residents who were considering job offers after graduation. Some were mulling over financially lucrative offers from an organization, even though they did not feel they had shared values and motivations with it. In the end, the residents who were faced with these decisions decided to go with a less financially rewarding practice but one with which they did have shared values and commitments. Another example is of a PA who went into the field of orthopedics, lured and seduced by the amount of money they could get paid. They were miserable. After a time, they transferred into family medicine, a better fit with what they truly valued. Looking back on my decision to go into endocrinology, it was based upon the nationally and internationally recognized leaders in the field, the amazing physiology and pathophysiology of the varied diseases, and the challenge of treating people with endocrinopathies. Though I recognized that I would be near the bottom of the physician pay scale, so much of endocrinology aligned with what I intrinsically valued.

Admittedly, it was seductive to consider higher salaries in other areas of medicine. However, practicing in those areas did not align with my personal intrinsic motivators.

One caution about people who are strongly wed to their own intrinsic motivators. They can be impatient with people that don't share similar values or have similar beliefs or even abhorrent when someone does something extra because of extrinsic motivation like more money instead of that it's the right thing to do. Examples could be not trusting another clinician, nurse, or student because you don't think they work as hard as you or don't seem to care as much as you do about patients, even though they still might have the correct idea or answer to a particular problem you are trying to resolve or put off when someone asks how much extra you are going to pay them before agreeing to cover for another who is out sick.

In addition to logic, emotions, and intrinsic motivation, adding optimism to your decision-making can be very valuable to helping you make the right decision and keeping you in your zone. Optimism is believing that the decision you made will work out, and if it doesn't, you'll figure out another way to make sure it does. Side benefits of optimism, according to Martin Seligman, a well-known psychologist who wrote *Learned Optimism*, are that people who are optimistic are more likely to have better health with less stress, stronger immune systems, are less likely to suffer from depression or cardiac disease, have higher self-esteem, better relationships, more successful careers, make more money, and live longer.[7] People like being around authentic, sincere optimists. They are upbeat, positive influencers, open to ideas, innovative, creative, agile with solutions, and able to overcome setbacks more easily. And the beautiful thing about being optimistic is that being so is only a decision away. You can decide to be optimistic or not. How do you do it?

Consider these following two suggestions from Six Seconds to enhance your optimism. First, challenge your thinking and recognize that failure is often Temporary, Isolated, and based on Effort (TIE). It requires one to understand that failure is temporary and not permanent (this will pass); is isolated and not pervasively affecting all aspects of one's life (this is only one area being affected); and requires additional effort (one has power over the situation and can do something about it).

The second suggestion is the three Ps: is the situation *permanent, pervasive,* and do you have *power* to make a change? As an example, take a student who failed their exam. Are they permanently a failure? Is everything they do a failure? Do they have the power to make efforts to not fail again? Of course, the answer is that it's just one test, not pervasive, and not a reflection on all they have accomplished already. They can make efforts and adjustments to reduce the chance of failing tests in the future. What example(s) can you come up with that test your optimism? Can you use the TIE, PPP strategy in those examples? Here are a couple of additional strategies to enhance your optimism.

1. Interview a colleague or friend or read about someone who has an inspiring story to tell, learning how they beat the challenges. Michael Jordan, one of the greatest basketball players of all time, summed it up best when he said, "I've missed more than 9,000 shots in my career. I've lost almost 300 games. Twenty-six times I've been trusted to take the game-winning shot and missed. I've failed over and over again in my life. And that is why I succeed."[8]

2. Exaggerate the pessimistic view to a humorous extreme. As an example, my book on managing health care's pain points finally gets published, but it's released on the same day the US government surprises everyone with radical and instantaneous changes to the health-care system that solve all medical professionals' stressors and makes my book immediately obsolete.

One caution about being optimistic, especially if one has a lower ability for logical thinking, is that one can be too optimistic. An example might be a clinician being too cavalier with their medical or surgical decisions including diagnosis and treatment plans. Consider the surgeon, cardiologist, or gastroenterologist who is overly optimistic/confident that they can be successful with any procedure, getting themselves in over their head and not considering assistance with a difficult case. Or think of the internist who forges ahead, anchored in believing that their diagnosis and treatment plan is correct, even if all the pieces of the diagnostic puzzle don't come neatly together, with complicated and confusing test results. Or a nurse who believes they can transfer a patient alone without the need for "a second." Or maybe the student who believes they know the material and don't feel the need to study.

Being too optimistic can lead to poor decision-making by causing people to underestimate risks, overlook potential problems, and not adequately prepare for negative outcomes. This can potentially lead to issues like neglecting important precautions, overconfidence in risky situations, and failure to recognize red flags in one's personal or professional life. This is often referred to as "optimism bias" or "unrealistic optimism" and can hinder effective problem-solving and planning.

One last caution about being too optimistic is that it can lead to "toxic positivity," a situation that makes a person think that feeling some level of sadness is unacceptable. Anecdotally, even before I knew about the term "toxic positivity," I thought about this when I was around someone who seemed too optimistic and overly happy. What are they hiding or suppressing, I thought? It didn't seem natural. Typically, as it turns out, they are suppressing emotions such as disappointment, melancholy, or sorrow rather than understanding and managing them in real time. Suppressing these emotions can lead to emotional outbursts and contribute to irritability, anxiety, and depression. It's like trying to stuff all these suppressed feelings into a closet. Eventually, the closet gets so filled with the emotion that it bursts open, typically at the wrong time in front of the wrong person.[9]

Recall from an earlier chapter that emotions are information that is trying to tell you something. The question again is, Are you listening? If so, after identifying, recognizing, and understanding where the emotions are coming from, the emotionally intelligent person can use those emotions for energy to assess the choices to resolve the issue, then make the best decision, rather than suppressing the emotions, hoping they go away and don't resurface.

One of the strategies I used in medical school was to ask myself "so what" about the medical condition I was studying. For example, "so what" if the person had a myocardial infarction, or "so what" if their kidneys or liver failed? It forced me to better understand the outcome of the malady and the impact to the patient. Similarly, I ask myself, "so what" if someone is good at self-management?

Here is the answer. People who are good at managing themselves are much more likely to stay in their zone and have it wider and longer because they have made better decisions for themselves. This begs the question, did you stay in your zone and have it wide because you made good decisions, or did you make good decisions because you were in your zone? It's the old chicken-or-the-egg analogy, though in the end what matters most is that you are in your zone, and blood flow to your logical brain is optimal, which allows you to make your best, most effective decisions. (Here, recall Chapter 4, on the neurophysiology of being in your zone.)

One last pearl to share about good self-management, and emotional intelligence in general, is that your psychological and emotional health benefits your physical health. How so? A meta-analysis from 2020 authored by Sarrionandia and Mikolajczak showed that people with higher EQ are more apt to make intentional decisions that lead to better sleep patterns, healthier nutritional habits, more physical activity, less substance usage, and, in general, lower levels of stress and the production of stress hormones like cortisol.[10] This meta-analysis confirms what many people already might intuitively know—that is, a healthy body is often a reflection of a healthy mind. And now that you know more about EQ, you can appreciate how a healthy mind is nurtured by emotional intelligence.

Putting EQ into Action

Read the following scenarios and ask yourself the following: *I want to make the best decision for myself, professionally and personally, so which components of decision-making would be helpful to make my decision?*

1. You were offered a leadership position in your organization, which requires you to give up much of your clinical work, which you are still enjoying, and oversee a large group of practitioners, nurses, and students. It is not something that you have done before or are trained to do, though you are curious and excited about the possibilities and opportunities of leadership and implementing your vision for the future.

2. You're a nurse who witnessed a physician, with whom you work closely, make a significant error then try to cover it up. You are trying to decide if you should bring it to the attention of an oversight group or keep it quiet.

3. You're a health-care student who is considering different job opportunities after graduation, weighing where the jobs are located, the other people who work there, the culture of the organization, and the amount of remuneration.

Chapter Takeaways

1. Self-management is all about recognizing the choices you have, being intentional with your decisions and the timing of those decisions (in your zone or not). The best decisions are typically made combining logic with emotions, along with being optimistic, in conjunction with what intrinsically motivates you.

2. It's ideal to know which decisions can be made quickly and which need to be made more slowly, requiring more thought.

3. Self-management is how you show yourself to other people, what you do and what you say. It's how your reputation is formed.

4. Typically, the best decisions are made when they are in alignment with how you think and feel and knowing what you want and want to avoid.

5. High-EQ people tend to have better psychological and physical health because of the decisions that they make.

Chapter 10

When You're Bumped Out of Your Zone (And You Will Get Bumped Out)

Instead of resisting any emotion, the best way to dispel it is to enter it fully, embrace it and see through your resistance.

—DEEPAK CHOPRA

In the process of writing this book, I got scammed. While innocently researching a health-care topic, like many of us do when we are trying to find information about a disease or medication we need to learn more about, I clicked on a website that resulted in a pop-up saying that my computer was now infected with a serious spyware, and I needed to call Apple security immediately using the posted number. I panicked.

Without going into the details, it went downhill from there. When I realized I had been scammed, I was max triggered. My amygdala was hijacked with a 911 alert. I was absolutely bumped out of my zone. I could feel the adrenaline and cortisol rushing and pulsating through my body. The disconnect between my limbic and rational brain couldn't have been greater. It was a chasm. I was in fight-or-flight mode. That's the bad news. The good news is that it tested every one of my emotional intelligence zone strategies and structure and . . . they worked. I got back in my zone.

First, I checked in with myself. Self-awareness is fundamental to EQ. I was out of my zone. I felt it physically (heart racing, breathing fast, muscles tight, clammy hands, head pounding) and emotionally. To acutely release this sudden hostility, I went to my old tried and true friend, cursing. I dropped f-bombs and even a few m-fs, not screaming them out loud but in privacy such that only I could hear them. While at first this might seem aggressive, inappropriate, and immature, there is science behind doing so. A 2023 study from Pakistan revealed that use of profane language had a significant inverse correlation with stress and anxiety and can do so by being a physical and emotional outlet allowing people to express their feelings without self-imposed limitations.[1] It's a way to provide a temporary release of tension and even give one a sense of power or control over a stressful situation. It works for me. Does it work for you?

Once I decompressed some, I then began using the "name it to tame it" strategy with the help of my emotional literacy knowledge. I wasn't just "angry," I was furious, livid, boiling, seething, betrayed, irate. I wasn't just "ashamed," I felt disgraced, dishonored, defamed, sorrowful, and violated. I wasn't just "sad," I was hurt, dejected, agonized and miserable. And I wasn't just "afraid" that the scammers were going to gain access to personal and financial information, I was frantic, petrified, and horrified.

The "name it to tame it" strategy was made famous by Dan Siegel, a psychiatrist, writer, and professor who is also the founding co-director of the Mindful Awareness Research Center at UCLA.[2] Based upon his research, the theory is that just saying the emotions activates the prefrontal cortex to allow one's mind to understand what the emotion is. Consciously labeling the intense emotions initiates a *physical* response by signaling the brain to send soothing neurotransmitters to the amygdala and the brain's emotional centers, calming your body and mind, and helping you to feel more in control. All this facilitates a decrease in emotional intensity to a level where you can then engage the rational part of your brain.[3] In this way, you can de-escalate from furious to upset to irritated—and it only takes a few seconds to achieve this shift. The key is recognizing that it just takes a conscious effort to deactivate your amygdala and activate your frontal lobes, the part of your brain responsible for rational, logical thinking. With this in mind, after I was scammed, I said, "I am so bumped out of my zone," and then named the many emotions I was feeling.

Next, I used the self-awareness power of recognizing patterns. Knowing that I had been in hijacked situations before and that with thoughtfulness and good self-management, including a heavy dose of optimism and recalling that situations tended to work out for me (though the lessons were painful), I remembered how I got myself back in the zone and started using the strategies that worked in the past, beginning with hitting the "pause button."

Pausing allowed my logical brain to catch up with my limbic brain, the proverbial count to ten, and gained some understanding about what I was feeling and why. Pausing gave me the chance to self-defuse the myriad of intense emotions I was feeling and deal with the situation without putting myself in circumstances that would bring regret, remorse, or worse. It's the difference between responding—allowing me to better understand what I can and cannot control—and reacting.

Reacting may have sent me even further down a road of no return. Pausing allowed me to recognize my choices and be intentional with my decisions so I could give myself time to employ some strategies to stay in my zone.

Additionally, to help me gain even better control of my emotions, I employed deep "box breathing" (breathe in for five seconds, hold for five seconds, breathe out for five seconds, hold for five seconds, and repeat). A 2017 study published in *Breathe* described the benefits of deep breathing on the respiratory, cardiovascular, and autonomic nervous systems and the cardiorespiratory unit.[4]

As I felt my heart slow along with my breathing, I made a conscious choice to be gracious, kind, and forgiving to myself. Yes, I told myself, I made a mistake that I regret; however, I will work through it and do the best I can to make things better. It was a bit of self-empathy that helped me better navigate my emotions and use them for energy to take action to secure my financial accounts and notify the authorities.

Despite taking these actions, it was difficult for me to sleep that night, replaying the events of the day. I was still somewhat wound up. So, I went back into my emotional toolbox for resourcing and grounding. Resourcing, for instance, is picturing a happy, calming place that you have been, or even imagined being, and the joy or calm of being there. For me it's a certain pool that I like to swim in and a particular mountain that I like to climb. What would yours be? Grounding is a relaxation technique that also distracts and calms. A common grounding strategy would be the 5-4-3-2-1 technique, where you look for five things that you can see, four things that you can touch, three things that you can hear, two things that you can smell, and one thing that you can taste. This combination helped me fall and stay asleep. (You can try them too!)

In the end, there was no negative outcome from the scam aside from the emotional break. I offered you this story for several reasons. First, we are all human and all vulnerable to people who use their intellectual abilities for malfeasance and can outsmart even the smartest of us. Second, we all can, and do, get triggered and bumped out of our zones. It's all part of being human. Third, I wanted to offer you a variety of strategies that you can use when you get bumped out of your zone. Note that there are no magic wands, silver bullets, or one-size-fits-all strategy that will help you get back in your zone if you are bumped out. What works for someone else might not work for you and vice versa.

Navigating Your Emotions and Keeping Your Zone Wide

Being able to navigate your emotions is another wonderful strategy to keep you in your zone and keep it wide. It's best to deal with an emotion while it's of low intensity, a tap on the shoulder. If the emotion is suppressed, ignored, not dealt with, it can grow over time from a pimple into a full-blown abscess. One of the rules of surgery is that "pus under pressure must be evacuated." In other words, the "abscess," your suppressed emotion, can rupture at any time and typically does so at the wrong time to the wrong person.

Consider the following. You're a clinician dealing with a multitude of patients during a routine day who have been complaining about the office staff, the parking, the cost of care, waiting too long to be seen, or not getting through on the phone. On top of that, their blood sugars are higher, blood pressures are creeping up, and kidney function is getting worse. Or you're a nurse who graciously came in on your day off to cover a twelve-hour shift for another nurse who "couldn't make it in that day." Then, before you know it, you are caring for more patients than you think is safe, they are sicker than you expected, and you don't have all the resources you need to correctly care for them. Or you're a health-care student on your clinical rotations at the hospital. Your patients are getting sicker during the day, but your preceptors are too busy to help and keep saying to you, "not now" though your patients are pushing you for answers "now." During all these interactions you feel more and more annoyed, but you kept suppressing the feeling, holding it all in. Then the last patient of the day, in each of those scenarios, gets mad at you because you weren't doing enough for them, not recognizing, appreciating, or caring about your herculean efforts to take care of everyone else that day. That's when you can't hold it in any longer. Pus under pressure must be evacuated, and all the pent-up, not-dealt-with anger from the day is unleashed and you dump all you've been suppressing on the person with whom you are now interacting. Think about how much easier it would have been to recognize the angry feelings during the day when the intensity was much lower—a tap on the shoulder, like feeling annoyed, perturbed, or irritated.

The first step in navigating your emotions goes back to the fundamentals of self-awareness and being emotionally literate, that is, being able to accurately recognize specifically what you are feeling. Annoyed? Perturbed? Livid? Enraged? Shame? Fear? There can be multiple feelings at the same time. The next step is determining what information those emotions are trying to tell you (hint: recall the definitions of the five basic emotions in Chapter 7). Next is how you can use these feelings as energy to make your next, hopefully intentional decision. Consider the example above when, during your day, you began feeling annoyed, perturbed, and irritated. Recognizing and understanding that these feelings were because of one of the scenarios listed above, you decide to take a few minutes' break in private to calm yourself, or you recognize that things are not in your control and move on (recognizing what you can and can't control), or you calmly discuss/vent the situations with your colleagues, staff, or peers, look for possible solutions to the situation, or you make some other intentional decision and use that feeling to take action rather than let it fester and eventually have it explode. The key is to be facile and flexible with your emotions, able to identify, recognize, and understand them. Then use that information as positive energy to be intentional with your decision and get what you want or need and stay away from what you don't want and don't need.

Throughout this chapter I have discussed how to get back in the zone once bumped out, and strategies to keep your zone wide when confronted with challenging emotions and situations. However, just as the best way to manage disease is to prevent it, the best way to prevent getting bumped out of your zone is to keep it as wide as often and as long as you can, right from the beginning. To do so, use the "emotional escalator."[5] This strategy begins with a close examination of your lifestyle. Here is how it works. Imagine an escalator, as shown in Figure 10.1.

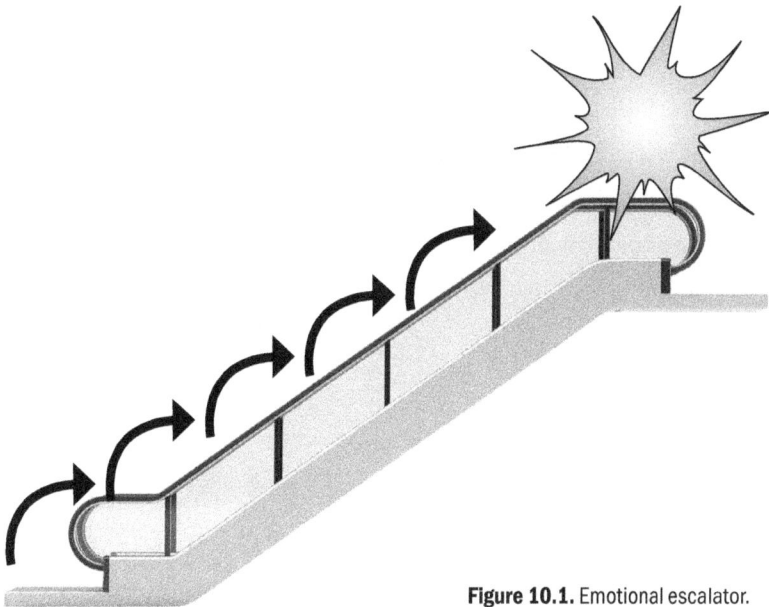

Figure 10.1. Emotional escalator.

Now answer the following "fun quiz" as truthfully as possible, scoring your responses between 1 and 5, with 1 representing "this is not me at all" and 5 meaning "this is definitely me":

1. I mostly eat whole foods—vegetables, fresh meat (beef, chicken, fish), grains, seeds, fruit, etc.

2. I sleep for a minimum of seven hours each night.

3. I have enough energy to fully live my life (e.g., I can get off the floor using just one hand).

4. I have a healthy weight, close to my target BMI.

5. I exercise regularly (e.g., walk briskly and do weight training for thirty minutes each) at least three times a week.

6. I feel connected to my family and friends.

7. I hardly ever feel lonely.

Now add up your scores:

- If you scored between 26 and 35, you are spending most of your life down near the bottom of the escalator, your zone is wide, and life is generally calm, stable, and undramatic. Most of the time, you are thoughtfully responsive, are able to self-manage, and navigate your emotions well, even when you are triggered.

- If you scored between 17 and 25, your zone is less wide and life is less calm and stable, as you live halfway up the escalator. Occasionally, you experience an amygdala hijack, more easily get bumped out of your zone, and may feel rotten afterward.

- If you scored between 7 and 16, your zone is likely very narrow, living your life one or two steps from the top of the escalator. You are easily triggered and frequently bumped out of your zone, reacting (vs. responding) most of the time. Amygdala hijacks are commonplace for you. Though you may think living here is completely normal, especially if your self-awareness is low, others might see you much differently, especially if your social awareness is also low. To them you may appear on edge, impatient, not open to their ideas or thoughts, or even unapproachable. Your patients might feel less safe if you look harried and rushed.

The emotional escalator exercise reminds me of the wisdom I tried to impart to my kids when they were growing up and heavily into their sports. That is, what gets you into the hall of fame is doing the basic things right, the fundamentals, and doing them consistently. Making a great play or doing something exceptional, once in a while, is great for the highlight film but not for the hall. The same holds true for how one lives their life.

The more you live your life near the bottom of the escalator, being consistent with a fundamental, healthy lifestyle, the more likely your zone will be wide, and the less likely you'll be triggered and bumped out of your zone. Additionally, you're more likely to thoughtfully respond once you become aware of the early signs of a hijack (rapid heartbeat, sweaty palms, clammy skin, goosebumps) and not just react.

Putting EQ into Action

Read the following scenarios and ask yourself: *How do I manage myself during this excruciating time?*

1. You are a clinician, stuck in standstill traffic and becoming very late to the office. You call your nurse, who informs you that the patients are piling up in the waiting room and getting very antsy because you aren't there and they are waiting so long.

2. You're a nurse, anxious to go home after working a grueling double shift. Exhausted, you begin frantically looking everywhere for your car keys and you can't find them.

3. You're a health-care student who needs to begin studying
   for your final exam. You look into your backpack, and your
   computer with all of your study material is gone and you can't
   remember where you left it.

Chapter Takeaways

1. We are all susceptible to having our amygdalae hijacked. The
   key is to have known strategies readily available to manage that
   hijack when it occurs and to recognize that what works for
   others might not work for you and vice versa.

2. It's best to navigate an emotion when it is of low intensity: a tap
   on the shoulder or a pimple. Suppressing the emotion allows
   it to intensify and become ready to explode, which typically
   happens at the worst time.

3. One of the best strategies for not getting bumped out of
   your zone is to keep it as wide as you can for as long as you
   can, using healthy lifestyles and being at the bottom of the
   emotional escalator.

Chapter 11

Relationship Management

*Do what you can to show you care about other people,
and you will make our world a better place.*

—ROSALYNN CARTER

Ask people how they would prefer to pass away, and the most common answer I hear is, "I want to be in my home, in my bed, without any pain and with all my close family and friends surrounding me." To me, this response is a litmus test, emphasizing the value and importance of relationships in people's lives and how they yearn for them during their lifetimes. Unfortunately, few things can be as complicated and complex as developing and maintaining relationships. Someone invariably says or does something that puts a wrench in the relationship, ultimately requiring an apology and healing or dooming it to destruction. I am so grateful for the countless fulfilling and enjoyable relationships over the years that have greatly enhanced my life, and still do, though I've also had a couple of fallings-out that were irreparable.

The one that stands out the most involved a longtime friend with whom I had many deep, meaningful conversations, shared experiences, and a business relationship. We were a team, challenging each other like Kahneman and Tversky, as described in Michael Lewis's book *The Undoing Project*,[1] to improve our subject matter, which centered around strategies to reduce clinician and nurse burnout and enhance wellness. I learned so much from my friend. We would then go on the road, traveling around New York State giving talks and workshops. It was successful and joyful on so many levels.

Then, suddenly, he stopped communicating with me, not taking my calls or responding to my texts or emails. It was also during the pandemic, so I couldn't just go over to his house and knock on his door. I was befuddled, clearly recognizing that I unwittingly did or said something that dramatically altered our friendship, though I wasn't sure what it was.

Then, about six months later, out of the blue he texted me, "If you want to know why I have distanced myself from you, call me," which I did in a heartbeat. He told me what I said that was so hurtful to him. I was mortified that I said what I did, though I did recall saying it and why. I apologized profusely for my comments. Had I known it would have caused this major rift in our relationship, I never would have said it. Ugh. Though some relationships can be repaired after a huge hiccup, ours ultimately failed despite attempts to repair it. We ultimately went our separate ways. I felt a deep hurt and loss and still do.

Relationships can be so challenging and difficult, yet still so important to have, i.e., can't live with them yet can't live without them. According to Northwestern Medicine psychologist and relationship expert Sheehan D. Fisher, good relationships promote reduced stress, better healing, healthier behaviors, greater sense of purpose, and longer life. Additionally, relationships are a cornerstone of happiness and living a full life because they provide support through rough times, keep us from being lonely, help us relate better with others, and can bring one great joy.[2]

According to the Harvard Study of Adult Development, which began in 1938 and longitudinally followed 724 people from all over the world on a biannual basis, what made people happy were positive relationships.[3] These positive relationships in turn keep us healthier, happier, and allow us to live longer. But the value of relationships doesn't stop there. Professional relationships are also valuable, providing increased collaboration, enhanced productivity, creativity, brainstorming, the transfer of knowledge, teamwork, enhanced morale, and the freedom to explore new opportunities.[4]

In health-care education specifically, there can be a variety of relationships that a student must be able to develop, maintain, and navigate. These include relationships with their professors and preceptors, classmates, staff, interdisciplinary teams, and patients during their clinical rotations. Developing and maintaining these relationships may offset the significant stress and anxiety inherent in these programs. To reduce the unavoidable stress and anxiety of education, according to the American Psychological Association, "Strong relationships with teachers and school staff can dramatically enhance students' level of motivation and therefore promote learning. Students who have access to more strong relationships are more academically engaged, have stronger social skills, and experience more positive behavior."[5]

Data from our longitudinal research done at the Le Moyne College PA program showed that PA students who had better relationships benefited in the following ways: (1) better grades at the end of their first year; (2) higher end-of-curriculum exam (EOCE) scores at the end of their second year; (3) higher scores on their certifying exam—the Physician Assistant National Certifying Exam (PANCE); (4) more "exceeds expectations" grades from their preceptors in social skills in the second year; (5) less burnout during their first year in PA school and feeling greater personal accomplishment during their second year. We also found that relationships mattered even more than overall and science undergrad grades in a student's success during PA school. Good relationships enhance the chance of success on a personal and professional level. The question is, though, how to do it.

I usually cringe when I hear someone say "you should" develop good, meaningful relationships with your family, friends, colleagues, staff, and patients. "You should" develop trust with them. Of course, those are good ideas. Given the complexity of people and all that we bring to an interaction and a relationship, the question remains, "How do we do it?"

When I was the senior medical quality director, I had a conversation with the CEO of a large health-care organization. It went like this:

"How do you get things done by the staff?" they asked.

"By developing and maintaining good relationships," I said.

"How do you develop good relationships?" they countered.

Scratching my head (figuratively), I answered, "Trust."

"How do you develop trust?" They dug deeper.

"With the five Cs," I replied, befuddled. "I try to display Competency, hoping people recognize and have confidence that I know what I am doing, and Consistency, I do it regularly. I show them that I truly and sincerely Care about their situation, which I do by generously listening and with curiosity, and I always circle back and Communicate with them what I found out and what we can do about resolving their concerns. In the end, I hope they see that I am a person of good Character, someone they can trust."[6]

This interaction had a big impact on me. If the CEO of a major health-care organization doesn't know how to develop relationships and trust to get things done, maybe it's not as well-known and as obvious as it seems. Maybe real guidance and education is needed on how to do it.

Indeed, maybe there is a structure with strategies that can be learned to educate even very smart, high-IQ, technically able people to get better at the soft skills, the social skills. Maybe it doesn't have to be "natural," based upon wit and instinct.

Back in 1964, Supreme Court Justice Potter Stewart was asked what the definition of pornography is. He famously replied that he might not be able to define it, but "I know it when I see it."[7] The same could be said for what good relationship management looks like. People who are very good at relationship management are typically very good at self- and social awareness and self-management. They are intentional with their decisions to develop, maintain, and enhance their relationships. They decide to be active, generous, and authentic listeners. When they listen, they are not merely waiting their turn to speak but rather listening to learn, first seeking to understand before trying to be understood. They listen with curiosity and not with judgment. They are fully present.

As they listen, they might use Susan Scott's suggestion in her book *Fierce Conversations*, which we discussed earlier.[8] They pay attention to *content* (what the person is talking about), *intent* (why the person is telling you this information), and *emotion* (what the person is feeling as they tell you their story). Lastly, active, generous listeners recognize their biases and take them into account when they eventually take their actions. According to Ten3 global internet polls, 82 percent of people would rather talk with a good listener than a good speaker.[9] I'd like to fashion myself as a generous listener and am amazed at how often I've been in conversation with someone who, at the end of the interaction, after me saying very little, said to me, "It's been great talking with you."

Great listeners listen with their eyes in addition to their ears. They consider all the nonverbal clues such as facial expressions and body language. They also listen closely to people's tone of voice, pitch, timbre, and volume. They are listening to not only what people are saying but how they are saying it. They recognize the value of Mehrabian's rule that 93 percent of communication is without the actual spoken word.[10] Great listeners also recognize that as they are looking at the person they are speaking with, the other person is also looking at them. Great listeners are aware of their thoughts and how those thoughts might show themselves in nonverbal communication via facial expressions or body language. In so doing, they let the speaker know that they are picking up what the other is putting down.

Finally, when it's time for the listener to speak, people who are good at relationship management are able to say the right thing, in the right tone, at the right time, to the right person. They speak directly with clarity and not in riddles. If someone tells them a story, rather than one-upping the other's story with their own story, they use the Six Seconds strategy to "VET" the other person's story: they **V**alidate, **E**xplore, then **T**ransform the person's story.[11] As an example, consider a patient who was telling you about a great vacation they took. Rather than respond-ing by telling them about your great vacation, VET their story: "That sounds so fun and exciting" (validate the emotion). Then explore the story further: "How did you decide to go there? What did you do there? What was the best part about it?" Lastly, transform by asking, "Would you go back there again? Would you recommend it to others? What are you thinking about for your next vacation?" I venture to say that many times people aren't telling you their story so that you can then tell them your story, though it happens seemingly all the time.

The following are a few scenarios that you might want to practice VETing. What would you say and do that would connect you to the storyteller (even more)?

- A friend of yours just told you about a trip that they took.

- A colleague told you of a great diagnosis that they made.

- A patient told you of a great loss that they recently suffered.

You may ask if there is guidance on what is the right thing to say. The answer is, yes! If you haven't read Dale Carnegie's book *How to Win Friends and Influence People*, I highly recommend it.[12] The book, written in the 1930s, remains relevant almost a century later. I came across the book early in my clinical practice when I realized that my new patients had many different types of personalities and brain preferences, and if I was going to be able to connect with them individually, I would have to up my game and enhance my relationship strategies. The book is filled with enjoyable anecdotes and relatable stories that are very practical, with concepts and strategies that should be obvious though often they are not. Dale Carnegie could have summarized his book with this quote: "When dealing with people, remember we are not dealing with creatures of logic. We are dealing with creatures of emotion."[13] This was obvious to him decades before Salovey, Meyer, and Goleman coined the phrase emotional intelligence. It appears that Mr. Carnegie "got it," and had high EQ before EQ was a thing.

Here are some specific strategies offered by Dale Carnegie to help you say the right thing at the right time to the right person.

- "Don't criticize, condemn, or complain.

- Give honest and sincere appreciation.

- Arouse in the other person an eager want.

- Talk in terms of the other person's interests.

- A person's name . . . is the sweetest and most important sound.

- Be a good listener. Encourage others to talk about themselves.

- Smile.

- Make the other person feel important.

- If you're wrong, admit it quickly and emphatically.

- Begin in a friendly way.

- Get the other person to saying 'yes, yes,' immediately.

- Let the other person do a great deal of the talking [and] feel like the idea is his or hers.

- Try honestly to see things from the other person's point of view and be sympathetic with [their] ideas and desires.

- Appeal to nobler motives."[14]

It's worth highlighting a few of these wonderful ideas offered by Dale Carnegie, beginning with knowing people's names. There are few things, if any, that are sweeter to someone than someone else saying their name. Conversely, someone not knowing their name or saying it incorrectly is like fingernails on a chalkboard to them. Knowing someone's name humanizes them, is a sign of respect, and confers importance. Upon entering an exam room and meeting a new patient for the first time, I would typically ask my new patient, "How would you like me to call you?" recognizing the value of someone's name and the correct way to pronounce it. Walking through the hospital, I would say hello to all the staff by name, from nurses and therapists to environmental services, security, and our patient transporters. Based upon their positive facial expressions, it was easy to see how they liked knowing that I cared enough about them to know their names.

The second highlight is offering an apology and the value of doing so. A true, sincere empathic apology that expresses remorse and humility may help mend a relationship and emotional wounds and restore trust. Apologizing for one's actions takes courage and bravery. It can be a very difficult and humbling experience that requires sacrificing one's ego. For clinicians and nurses, saying "I'm sorry" for a mistake they made has been a long-standing hot topic given the concern that saying you're sorry is an admission of guilt that will lead to a malpractice lawsuit and potentially harm the clinician's reputation. What to do may be summarized best by a quote by Dr. Tom Gallagher, Professor and Associate Chair of the Department of Medicine at the University of Washington, who has published extensively on disclosure of adverse events in medicine: "It is clear from the literature that being clear with patients and apologizing overall makes it less likely they will sue you." Additionally, full disclosure to patients may be associated with a lower chance of patients leaving their clinician, greater trust, and even less sanctions against the physician.[15]

The third highlight is being sincerely appreciative and grateful. This always reminds me of a famous quote from Albert Einstein: "There are only two ways to live your life. One is as though nothing is a miracle. The other is as though everything is a miracle."[16] I interpret "miracle" as being appreciative for the wonders of the world and having gratitude for the wonderful things that people do in the world, even if what they are doing seems routine. I witnessed one of the unit nurses interacting with a patient who was acting out in such a kind, caring, and compassionate way that after she de-escalated the situation, I had to let her know how awesomely she had managed the patient. Her face lit up with my sincere, genuine compliment. As I've gotten older and learned to take nothing for granted—everything is a miracle—thanking people for their time, efforts, and expertise at every opportunity has become the routine. It feels good for me to express my gratitude to them, and they feel good knowing that they are sincerely appreciated.

Here are some additional suggestions to enhance your relationship management, directly from Bradberry and Greaves' *Emotional Intelligence 2.0* book:

- "Be open and be curious.
- Enhance your natural communication style.
- Avoid giving mixed signals.
- Remember the little things that pack a punch.

- Take feedback well.

- Build trust.

- Have an 'open-door' policy.

- Only get mad on purpose.

- Don't avoid the inevitable.

- Acknowledge the other person's feelings.

- Compliment the [other] person's emotions or situation.

- When you care, show it.

- Explain your decisions, don't just make them.

- Make your feedback direct and constructive.

- Align your intention with your impact.

- Offer a 'fix it' statement during a broken conversation.

- Tackle a tough conversation."[17]

If you didn't get enough from those examples, here is a list of other phrases that can be used to help you say the right thing, helping you be more emotionally intelligent in your conversations and interactions. As written by Kathy and Ross Petras in a 2023 cnbc.com article, if you use these responses, you'll likely be thought of as having higher emotional intelligence.[18]

- "I'm so curious. Would you be willing to share more?"

- "Can you help me understand?"

- "I hear you." "I get what you are driving at."

- "I can see what you're saying, though I might see it from a different angle" or "I have a different perspective" or "my bias is . . ." (In short, saying I disagree with someone often makes people feel defensive and carries a load.)

- "How does that make you feel?"

- "Could you tell me more about what's wrong so I can better understand the problem?"

- "What do you mean?"

- "I appreciate your help."

- "You raise some helpful points, and I think we can work together here."

- "I'd love your input on this."

- "Are you open to some thoughts I have?" Or "Are you open to some observations I have?"

- "I'm concerned (confused, upset, worried, etc.) about the situation here."

- "I feel this way about . . ."

- "I'm sorry" or "I apologize."

- "Thank you!"

- "I welcome your thoughts." Especially in an email or text.

To put these high-EQ phrases into action, I offer my workshop attendees these scenarios and ask them which of the preceding comments might be useful to maintain their relationship. I offer the same exercise to you and a sample response (though feel free to consider alternative responses noted above or come up with your own original ones).

- Someone said or did something that angered you. You confront them.

  » Try, "Can you help me understand?"

- You're at a meeting and you disagree with someone about the topic being discussed.

> » Try, "I can see what you're saying, though I might see it from a different angle" or "I have a different perspective" or "My bias is . . ."

- You're in the exam room when your patient made an off-color comment about your religion, sexual preference, or something else very personal to you.

  > » Try, "What do you mean?"

- Someone did you a very big favor without you even asking them.

  > » Try, "Thank you!"

What is also valuable for a clinician or nurse, when speaking with a patient and determining the best words to use, is to gauge the health literacy of the patient with whom you are interacting and adjust the words accordingly. To emphasize the need for gauging a patient's health literacy, a friend of mine published a memoir entitled *The Book of David* (MindStir Media, 2025). The book is a beautifully written, heartfelt story of the author, Dr. Michael Gordon, and his relationship with his brother who had special needs and diabetes. In one of the chapters Michael describes how his brother David's endocrinologist verbally gave him medically sound instructions on managing his diabetes, though David had no idea what his doctor instructed him to do. Michael, recognizing that the instructions might be too complicated, asked his brother if he understood what the doctor told him. He replied, "I have no idea." Happily, the doctor gave it a second try and spoke with words that David could understand. Andrew Grove, an engineer and CEO, may have said it best: "How well we communicate is not determined by how well we say things but how well we are understood."[19] Special attention to this concept may be even more important with our patients who have special needs.

Checking for understanding after giving information to patients, termed "the teach back"—that is, asking the patient what they heard and understood from what was said to them—may also be very valuable. There are four steps for people to communicate the spoken word: what a person thinks they said, what they actually said, what a person thinks they heard, and what they actually heard. I use the teach back strategy frequently and am amazed and grateful at how well some patients heard and understood an explanation about their condition and how to manage it, while other times not so much, which requires me to give it another try.

One word of caution when using the spoken word to communicate: People usually pick up on insincerity and inauthenticity. Therefore, if you try to fake it, even if you are using the Dale Carnegie strategies or the phrases noted above, they will likely be suspicious of your intent. This is best summarized by the following quotes: "Sincerity is not to say everything you think but to mean everything that you say,"[20] and, per Brené Brown, "Authenticity is about the choice to show up and be real. The choice to be honest. The choice to let our true selves be seen."[21] People might also shy away from people who know it all and are arrogant. A dose of humility goes a long way toward likability and strong relationships. Saying the right thing at the right time is a wonderful skill, and just as important is writing the right thing at the right time, though that can be even more difficult.

The challenge with written communication is that the other person will not get the benefit of your voice or your body language and facial expressions. The person high in self- and relationship management skills tries to consider how the other person might read the written word before hitting the send button. I must admit that I have written and rewritten text messages and emails several times before sending, making sure they have the right message and tone I want to deliver, even without these physical cues. Additionally, whenever possible I do use some of the EQ phrases noted previously. In written correspondence, I will often end with, "I welcome your thoughts" if the topic is about ideas and decisions. I offer this to you as something that has worked for me. Maybe it might do the same for you? It's also valuable to hit your own internal pause button and get back in your zone or have it wider before responding to an aggravating, off-putting text or email, such as someone questioning or being critical of why you did something, or why they can't do something that you expected them to do.

There's a story about Abraham Lincoln that highlights this point. As the legend goes, Lincoln was angered about one of his general's actions. At first, he reacted by writing him a nasty letter. Then he paused, put the letter in his desk drawer, and thought that if he still felt that way the next day, he would send the letter. The next day he tore the letter up, never sending it, emphasizing the power of the pause and getting back in your zone before responding. If you did want to send a letter confronting the situation and you're in your zone, then following Susan Scott's idea in her book *Fierce Conversations* can be valuable. One can deliver a message to someone about something significant without it "carrying a load" that will evoke a negative reaction from another, such as making someone feel uncomfortable and defensive.[22] Pausing to craft a response that makes your point without making someone feel badly or gaslighting the situation, potentially putting a kink in the relationship, could make all the difference.

One last word about the written word worth noting. An article in *JAMA* came out in 2023 entitled "Comparing Physician and Artificial Intelligence Chatbot Responses to Patient Questions Posted to a Public Social Media Forum."[23] The question the article wanted to answer was, "Can an artificial intelligence chatbot assistant provide responses to patient questions that are of comparable quality and empathy to those written by physicians?" The short answer is yes, and with higher quality and more empathy, leading to a 78.6 percent preference for the chatbot responses over the physicians. This is a good/bad news story. The good news is that the chatbot may potentially be able to offload some physician workload and reduce the risk of burnout while also improving patient outcomes (more studies are needed). The bad news is that a computer was thought to be more human and empathic than a human! Maybe another reason for EQ training in health care.

If you are still looking for one more book on how to get to really, deeply know someone, consider the heartfelt and beautifully written *How to Know a Person: The Art of Seeing Others Deeply and Being Deeply Seen*, by David Brooks.[24] Brooks describes how he evolved over time, allowing himself to "really feel." By connecting with himself on a deeper level, he was able to more deeply connect with others, bringing to life the saying, "To connect with others, one must first connect with themselves." Once he did so, he was able to see people in their struggles and their strengths, which brought significant meaning and benefit to his relationships and his life.

One of the questions my workshop attendees raise is, How do you know if you connected with someone? Good question with a simple answer: emotions. To emphasize the point, I go on to retell the story of *The Celestine Prophecy*, a novel by James Redfield that in essence asks the question, What is the most important thing in life? Spoiler alert: Relationships. Surprise!

Redfield, in his description of an interaction between two people, puts a physical energy field around them, and one of three results can happen. (1) Someone sucks away all the energy field from the other, leaving them depleted as the other person walks away feeling great. (2) Vice versa can also occur. I suspect both scenarios have happened to us all at some time in our lives. (3) The best outcome, however, is when the physical energy fields of both people in the interaction come together such that at the end of the conversation, both walk away with greater levels of energy, feeling even better than when they entered the conversation. That's when you know you connected.

I opened this chapter by saying that relationships are complex and complicated, and used examples to highlight my point. However, I think that after all is said and done, relationships don't have to be as complicated as they are if we all recognize that most people just want five things from an interaction: to be seen, heard, understood, valued, and appreciated. That's it. Simple.

Now, interestingly, if I take the first letter of each word and make an acronym, it spells the word "SHUVA." What is enlightening to me is that SHUVA is the Hebrew word for "return." In essence, what people want "in return" from us during any interaction is SHUVA. So, if you are with another person and the interaction is beginning to get complicated and complex, simplify it, remembering to return to them what they deep down really want and need.

Putting EQ into Action

Read the following scenarios and ask yourself: *Given the strategies outlined in this chapter, how would I discuss, or write to, the other person involved in my story to try to maintain my relationship with them?*

1. You're a clinician sharing a case with another clinician when you have a disagreement about the management that gets heated. Both of you walk away, mad at the other.

2. You're a longtime nurse in a clinic or on a hospital unit when a new nurse becomes part of your team whom you find irritating and hard to work with.

3. You're a student in a health-care education program and you receive an email from another student that you feel is inappropriate and tweaks you.

Chapter Takeaways

1. Many, if not most of us, yearn for solid relationships, though they can be very complicated and complex to maintain. However, the right skill set, including active, generous, curious listening with our ears and eyes and saying the right thing at the right time to the right person in the right place, can increase the likelihood of success.

2. Just like emotional intelligence being a competency, one can learn how to develop and maintain relationships.

3. Don't forget to "VET" a person's story. It will drive connection with them.

4. It might be difficult to define what a great relationship is, though one may know it when they see it, or feel it.

5. What is not complicated about developing and maintaining relationships is simply that what people desire "in return" from you is to be seen, heard, understood, valued, and appreciated: SHUVA.

Chapter 12

Self-Direction and Empathy

We cannot tell what may happen to us in the strange medley of life.
But we can decide what happens in us—how we can take it,
what we do with it—and that is what really counts in the end.

—JOSEPH FORT NEWTON

When my son, an introspective, insightful, and very thoughtful person, was a teenager and trying to figure out life, he looked me straight in the eye and asked me a pointed question: "Dad, what do you really want out of life?" It made me pause and think deeply about the answer. Given that life was hectic at that time—practicing medicine with all its ups and downs, caring for two teenagers with all their ups and downs, being a good husband and co-managing the house with my wife, whose life was similarly busy as a full-time attorney—my short answer to my son was, "Shalom. Peace." That's what I really wanted then, and even today. Not only for me and my life but for all who live in the world.

Unwittingly, my son had asked me an astute question about my self-direction, which by definition is the ability to direct or guide oneself, to make choices for or by oneself, ideally in alignment with what you really want and want to avoid.[1] It's about what gives you meaning and purpose, your North Star. As Oprah Winfrey said, "There is no greater gift you can give to yourself than to honor your calling. It's why you were born and how you become truly alive."[2] But I believe self-direction is more than that. Self-direction is also about what we want and don't want each day, such that at the end of our day, if we reflect on the day's events, we will be able to say, "That was a good day."

A partner in my wife's law practice was famous for saying to his children each day as they left the house for school, "Have a productive day." Being productive is what he truly valued and what gave him meaning and purpose, and it showed in how hard he worked.

Self-direction is also about what we want with each interaction. Susan Scott raises these question in her book *Fierce Conversations*: What is the emotional wake you want to leave behind after interacting with another? What do you want them to think of you, and what do you want them to think of the organization you are representing?[3]

How to Know What You Want and Don't Want

How do you know what you want and don't want? First, reflect on what truly gives you meaning and purpose and why. Many of us go on autopilot. I took that reflective step for the first time late in my professional career. The question I needed to answer was, what truly gave me meaning and purpose? It was important to me to ponder this question as I was getting older and wasn't sure how much time, energy, and health

I would have in the future to achieve what I wanted professionally. I wanted to make good decisions and not waste time going off in the wrong direction. My answer, in addition to "shalom," was *tikkun olam*, a Hebrew expression that translates to "repair the world." It means leave the world better than you found it, even if it's just my little corner of the world in my little community. I was immediately challenged on my decision when I was offered a relatively high-paying position reviewing physician documentation relative to billing. But since it didn't "feel" like it met my criterion of tikkun olam, I declined it.

What professional positions did meet my tikkun olam criterion? Continuing to practice medicine in my role as an endocrine hospitalist and leader of our hospital's diabetes program. I also became the medical director of a local physician assistant program, educating some future practitioners while also researching the impact of EQ on PA students. I also took on the role of chief medical officer of a transportation company, assisting Medicaid enrollees to get to their health-care appointments. I also became the Jewish ambassador within our local Jewish community and formed a group called the Council of Jewish Organizations (COJO) that brought together lay and professional leadership each month to discuss issues that impacted our local community while also trying to grow it. What is the connection among all these seemingly disparate positions?

It's the answer to my "why," which is "Living to Give," a slogan from the book *Wonder Drug* by Drs. Stephen Trzeciak and Anthony Mazzarelli.[4] The book describes the seven scientific benefits of individuals who serve others. I made my decisions before the book came out, since all I knew was that it felt good for me to *give* instead of take. As a clinician I could *give* patients over thirty years of clinical experience and *give* them better health and improvement of their acute medical conditions. Additionally, given that 30 percent of the patients who enter our hospital have diabetes, I believed that the right thing to do was to *give* them the best diabetes care we could in our hospital to reduce their risk of complications and readmissions. As the PA medical director, I could *give* education, both tech and touch, to the next generation of clinicians. With our research, I could *give* additional insight into the value of EQ on health-care student education. As the CMO, I could *give* insights to our leadership team as to the challenges facing health-care practitioners and assist streamlining the process of filling out required forms to ensure that the most medically vulnerable in our society can get to health-care offices, clinics, and hospitals to prevent disease or treat it. By doing so and taking a pebble out of the shoes of medical practitioners, it might make a hard day easier and reduce the risk of burnout. As the Jewish ambassador I could *give* to my community, helping to sustain and even grow Jewish engagement in our synagogues and institutions, ensuring its survival. I share my story hoping that it might assist you in discovering your own why.

An exercise that Six Seconds suggests to help you find your North Star is to imagine that a famous movie producer wants to make a movie about you to inspire the next generation.[5] What would you want your movie to be about, and what would its title be? It may be revealing to have this conversation with people who are close to you. I suspect you will learn much about them, and them about you, in a very short time.

Another exercise suggested by Six Seconds is constructing your own personal Hall of Fame.[6] Here's how to do it. First answer, "Who in the world and in your life do you wish to emulate?" Make a book or poster with photos and descriptions including the one quality that qualifies each person to enter this honored status. Then, make a statement on the cover of the book or at the top of the poster that captures the criteria of this Hall of Fame. Finally, consider what you will need to do to qualify for your own Hall of Fame and act on it.

The last exercise to help you achieve your noble goal asks the following questions. What barriers do you have to overcome to pursue your noble goal? If you are not pursuing it, what is getting in your way? Are the barriers surmountable? If so, when can you now begin pursuing your noble goal? How would achieving your noble goal impact your life, professionally and personally?

Steve Jobs, the founder of Apple, used to ask, "If today was the last day of your life, would you want to do what you are about to do?"[7] Charlie Munger, Warren Buffett's longtime business partner, answered this question with "Go to bed smarter than when I woke up."[8] My answer would be, whatever I am going to do each day I hope to be productive, bring some modicum of peace and harmony to the people I interact with and the world at large, and make each person I interact with feel seen, heard, understood, valued, and appreciated. What do you want each day? And maybe equally as important, what don't you want each day? Knowing the answers to these questions again helps you make decisions and keeps you in your zone and keeps it wide.

Emotional Intelligence Helps with Crucial Conversations

As health-care professionals, we frequently have what are called crucial conversations, or what I like to call adult conversations. Defined by Patterson, Grenny, McMillan, and Switzler in *Crucial Conversations: Tools for Talking When Stakes Are High*, a crucial conversation takes place when the stakes are high and there are opposing opinions and emotions are strong.[9] People with high EQ don't typically run away from these potentially confrontational discussions; they just tend to be better at having them. This is because they are able to recognize if they are in their zone prior to the conversation. If they are not, they get themselves into their zone, using strategies described previously, and proceed. They also are socially aware, knowing if the person they are interacting with is in their zone or not, and adjusting to that. They also recognize that timing is everything. High-EQ people are very aware of what they want and don't want during the conversation, and they self- and relationship-manage accordingly.

Here's an example. As a medical quality director trying to reduce hospital-acquired infections and conditions, I had to talk with the chief of neurosurgery about our nurses and staff observing that he was not washing his hands when he went into patients' rooms at the hospital. What I wanted was to inform him of these observations and have him change his behaviors. What I didn't want was to make him feel defensive or angry at the nurses or staff who blew the whistle on him or upset with me for confronting him about this issue. Thus, in a quiet place when he had a free moment and was in his zone, I asked him if he had time and was open to hearing some observations the nurses and staff had. He agreed and I informed him about the concern, then sought to understand his point of view while actively listening without judgment. Then, being mindful of my tone, I asked him if he recognized that people considered him a role model and if there were any barriers to his washing his hands prior to going into the rooms that we could help him overcome. In the end, he thanked me for addressing the issue with him in the way that I did. I achieved what I wanted and avoided what I didn't want.

During my workshops I offer the attendees the following scenarios, asking them to consider what they want and don't want with each situation. I offer this to you and ask you the same question. How would you answer?

- You have to let a patient know that you made a mistake.
- You have to give "bad news" to a patient.
- A patient gave you a gift.
- Your direct report gave you a negative evaluation.
- Your friend told you a great story about their vacation.

- You're faced with studying for a test or going out with friends/family.
- Someone said something negative about you to someone else and you found out.

Self-direction is all about making decisions in alignment with what you want and don't want. By doing so, you will make better decisions and stay in your zone while keeping it wide. It may do the same for the person or persons with whom you are interacting, while strengthening your connection with them. Make no mistake, connecting with others is powerful, and maybe the most potent connector of people is empathy.

Life is hard. Most, if not all of us, can't get through it by ourselves. Empathy is the magic, powerful ingredient that connects us with each other, and helps us each navigate life a little easier. Brené Brown, an expert in empathy, has noted that "empathy is a choice, and it's a vulnerable choice, because in order to connect with you, I have to connect with something inside myself that knows that feeling."[10] You don't need to have the same situation or scenario as another, you just must have had the same feeling. We all know what pain feels like, even if we didn't break a bone. We all know what sadness feels like, even if we didn't have the same loss, and we all know what shame and guilt feel like, even if we didn't make the same mistake. By empathizing with another, you are connecting with them. As Leo Buscaglia, an American author, motivational speaker, and professor in the Department of Special Education at the University of Southern California, wrote, "Too often we underestimate the power of a touch, a smile, a kind word, a listening ear, an honest compliment, or the smallest act of caring, all of which have the potential to turn a life around."[11] In fact, feeling *with* someone might be the most powerful way to connect with another.

The value of empathy, especially in health care, goes beyond connecting with another. Dano Moreno, the CEO of CivCom and a children's book author, notes that patients benefit from empathic providers by having reduced pain and mortality, fewer medical complications, improved immune complications, decreased health-care utilization and costs, and improved medication adherence. Clinicians also benefit by having better patient and job satisfaction, less burnout and absenteeism, and increased levels of patient trust.[12]

There are also financial benefits to compassion and empathy, as described by Trzeciak and Mazzarelli in their book *Compassionomics*.[13] As examples, these include increased patient satisfaction, which increases patient loyalty and word-of-mouth referrals, while also improving hospital ratings and reputation, which in turn leads to more revenue as more patients want care in those organizations. This also helps retain staff, who want to work at a reputable institution that gives them pride, resulting in reduced staff turnover and the associated savings. Additionally, when people feel cared for, they are more likely to be adherent with their treatment plans and therefore less likely to suffer costly complications or suffer readmissions because of non-compliance. When people feel cared for, they are also less likely to sue their practitioners, leading to fewer malpractice claims and those associated costs.

Now that I perhaps have convinced you of the value of empathy, the question remains: Can someone learn to be more empathic (spoiler alert: Yes!) and if so, how do you do it?

People have commonly defined empathy as walking in someone else's shoes. It's seeing with the eyes of another, listening with the ears of another, and feeling with the heart of another. Maybe this was best summarized by Stephen Covey, who said, "When you listen with empathy to another person, you give that person psychological air."[14] More specifically, however, the elements of empathy align with the elements of EQ, and like EQ, empathy is a competency that you can get better at with desire and effort.

The first competency is self- and social awareness, the ability to "pick up what the other person is putting down," recognizing what they are thinking and feeling because you have thought and felt the same feeling, even if you have not experienced the same situation. Pain is pain. Sadness is sadness. Frustration is frustration, despite the circumstances that might have precipitated the emotion and feelings of each.

The second competency is self-management, which means that you have choice. You can choose compassion or not. If you choose compassion, do you choose sympathy or empathy? (There is a big difference, which I will address below.) Once you have decided to be empathic, the third and last element is self-direction. That is, you *want* to let the other person know that you picked up what they put down, and you communicate back to them either verbally, while being aware of the intonation of your voice, or nonverbally, with facial expressions, body language, or with an appropriate physical gesture like putting your hand on their shoulder or elbow. Ideally, the response needs to be made with curiosity and not with judgment. A response such as "Why did you do that, what were you thinking?" with an indignant tone will cause disconnection and not the desired connection. The other person might become defensive and shut down, not telling you any more then, or maybe ever again. Additionally, trying to cheer someone up who is depressed or grieving is often unsuccessful.

Many times, people need to have their moment to express their emotions and feelings. To see these elements of empathy in action, I invite you to watch a brilliant two-minute video clip from a wonderful Pixar movie entitled *Inside Out*. The scene is "Sadness Comforts Bing Bong."[15] Joy cannot make Bing Bong feel better by trying to cheer him up when he is down. Sadness, genuinely empathizing with Bing Bong using the strategies just described, allows him to move on after he experienced a serious loss.

Most people aren't telling you their story so that you can tell them your story. Unfortunately, when I listen to one person tell another person their story, the usual response for the person receiving the story is to immediately tell them their story. This is a missed opportunity to learn more about the original story and what the person was thinking, feeling, their motivations, and more by using the VET strategy: **V**alidate the person's feelings; **E**xplore what they might be thinking and feeling; **T**ransform by inquiring how they are thinking about their next steps.

Many times, people aren't telling you their story for you to fix the issue either. In our family, my kids especially, who have been well schooled in this regard, will begin telling my wife and me about an issue and preface the story by saying, "I'm not looking for your advice or for you to fix this. I just want to tell you the situation." Or if they don't preface it that way before we respond to their concerns, we ask, "Would you like our advice or did you just want to tell us what happened?" Brené Brown, describing the difference between sympathy and empathy, has a great empathic response to someone who is telling another their story of woe: "I don't even know what to say. I'm just so glad you told me."[16] Try it. I have and I can immediately feel the connection with another.

The Challenges of Empathy: Compassion Fatigue and Selectivity

There are several challenges to being empathic. Consider the following. How can empathy be sustained when the stress level is high, and we are suffering from our own compassion fatigue, which is "the physical and mental exhaustion and emotional withdrawal experienced by those who care for sick or traumatized people over an extended period of time"?[17] This experience can make our tank empty with nothing left to give, make our zone narrow, or bump us out of it. How do we maintain and display empathy with an empty emotional tank?

And what about being selective with our empathy, offering it to some but not to others, based on biases that we all have?[18] Here is an example of potential selective empathy you might be able to relate to. A person with alcohol or substance use disorder keeps coming back to the hospital with self-sabotaging behaviors like alcohol intoxication or overdoses. You patch them up then send them on their way, the proverbial "treat 'em and street 'em." The level of empathy one might have for this person might be very different than for a person who develops a malignancy like acute myelogenous leukemia, especially as a child, through no fault of their own. Your empathy might be for one and not for another. The question is, How do you overcome these empathy challenges of compassion fatigue and being selective?

The answer is self-awareness: It's knowing and recognizing that you are exhausted, depleted, and have these selective biases, and recognizing that the patient, the *person*, a human being, has a story that allowed for that unfortunate situation and condition. Truth be told, everyone has a story, their own personal journey, as to how they got to where they are in life at the time you are seeing them.

To emphasize that everyone has a story, I invite you to watch a profound and compelling video produced by the Cleveland Clinic entitled "Empathy: The Human Connection to Patient Care."[19] The video shows patients, caretakers, health-care practitioners, nurses, and others in a variety of situations, and reveals an underlying story of each person that is not visible on the surface. For instance, a young man walking, struggling down a long hallway, using a walker, grimacing in pain after suffering from a car accident, is accompanied by the text, "Worried about how he will pay for this." A mother and daughter walk out of a loved one's room, holding each other up, with tears streaming down their faces with the caption saying, "They just signed a DNR." Or an older woman sitting in the waiting room of the mammography center with a worried, pensive look, with the caption reading, "They saw 'something' on her mammogram." And maybe the most heartbreaking scenario for me was a mother and her young daughter walking through the hospital, with the caption reading, "Husband is terminally ill. Visiting dad for the last time." This video highlights that, beneath the surface of what we might see and hear from someone, there is an underlying, untold story that we can only access if we inquire. Knowing that story may make all the difference in how we think about another, connect with them, manage ourselves, and manage their medical conditions.

If watching the video wasn't enough to convince you that everyone has a story to tell, consider this. A young man who suffered from a horrible, unremitting substance use disorder repeatedly came back to the hospital overdosed, then withdrawing. The distraught and frustrated medical residents who were responsible for his care would say, "Geez, he's back. We'll patch him up and he'll just come back again. What a waste of time." As the story goes, one day, a new attending physician came on service. She heard the residents' account of the patient's history, then decided to take a different approach to the case. She, with the residents trailing behind her, went into the patient's room, introduced herself, sat down, and asked the patient a pointed question: "Mr. Jones, when did you first recognize that you were addicted?" Mr. Jones sighed, paused, then told his story of the challenges that he faced growing up, in poverty with a broken home filled with domestic, sexual, and physical violence and drug use. From that point forward, the residents had a very different feeling for Mr. Jones, a feeling of empathy. Now that they knew his story, they could now feel *with* him. My point is that everyone has a story, and if we pause long enough, taking the time to listen to it with curiosity and without judgment, we might have a different way to feel *with* someone.

It's worth mentioning the Adverse Childhood Events (ACE) study here, since "Mr. Jones" is not alone in dealing with his adult addiction after suffering multiple traumas as a child. The Centers for Disease Control (CDC) and Kaiser Permanente conducted this study in the mid-1990s, surveying 17,000 patients. What they found is that there was a direct correlation between childhood physical, sexual, and emotional abuse and neglect and household dysfunction such as divorce, violence, substance abuse, mental illness, incarceration, adult onset of chronic diseases, employment challenges, and premature death. The higher the number of adverse childhood events, the greater the incidence of negative future outcomes.[20] It might be worthwhile for clinicians, nurses, and those in training who care for adult patients to be familiar with this information so they can better understand the "why" behind the "what" of patients' diseases and behaviors.

Empathy versus Sympathy: A Big Diff

Sympathy is feeling *for* someone. Empathy is feeling *with* someone. People often feel like they are being empathetic when they are in reality expressing sympathy. A prime example is when someone has suffered a loss of some type, whether it be a person, a pet, or an object. The common expression is "I am sorry for your loss." Some might interpret this expression as the person with the loss being a victim, with the sympathizer's subconscious subtitle really saying, "I'm sorry for your loss. I'm glad it wasn't my loss." Personally, that's the feeling I had when people tried to console me after my mom passed away. I deeply appreciated and recognized their kindness and concern, though I had to look past their feeling *for* me, like I was a victim. From my perspective, I would have much preferred to be "VETed" by concerned family, friends, and acquaintances. What would you rather hear if you were the person on the receiving end: "I'm sorry for your loss" or "That must be so hard to lose your mom. Can you tell me about her?" Again, per Brené Brown, "Empathy drives connection whereas sympathy drives disconnection."[21] Therefore, empathy might be considered a higher level of compassion than sympathy.

If you are looking for even more ways to express empathy, consider the responses in Figures 12.1 and 12.2, from the Department of Veterans Affairs.[22]

Empathetic Responses

NAMING	UNDER-STANDING	RESPECTING	SUPPORTING	EXPLORING	"I WISH"
This must be ... • Frustrating • Overwhelming • Scary • Difficult • Challenging • Hard	What you just said really helps me understand the situation better.	I really admire your ... • Faith • Strength • Commitment to your family • Thoughtful-ness • Love for your family	We will do our very best to make sure you have what you need.	Could you say more about what you mean when you say ... • I don't want to give up • I am hoping for a miracle	I wish we had a treatment that would cure you (make your ill-ness go away). [Remember, we do not have palliative treat-ments to offer the patient]
I'm wondering if you are feeling ... • Sad • Scared • Frustrated • Overwhelmed • Anxious • Nervous • Angry	This really helps me better under-stand what you are thinking.	You (or your dad, mom, child, or spouse) are/is such a strong person and have/has been through so much.	Our team is here to help you with this.	Help me under-stand more about ...	I wish I had better news.
It sounds like you may be feeling ...	I can see how dealing with this might be ... • Hard on you • Frustrating • Challenging • Scary	I can really see how (strong, dedicated, loving, caring, etc.) you are.	We will work hard to get you the support that you need.	Tell me more ...	I wish the situation were different.
In this situation some people might feel ...	I can see how important this is to you.	You are such a (strong, caring, dedicated) person.	We are com-mitted to help you in any way we can.	Tell me more about what (a miracle, fighting, not giving up, etc.) might look like for you?	I wish that for you too. [In response to what a patient or family member wishes, such as a miracle]
I can't even imagine how (name emotion) this must be.	Dealing with this illness has been such a big part of your life and taken so much energy from you.	I'm really impressed by all that you've done to manage your illness (help your loved one deal with their illness).	We will be here for you.	Can you say more about that?	I wish we weren't in this spot right now.

Figure 12.1. Empathetic responses. (Adapted from and made available for public use through a US Department of Veterans Affairs contract with VitalTalk, Order No. VA777-14-P-0400.)

Responses to Challenging Questions

God's going to bring me a miracle:
• I hope that for you too. (Remember, no buts!) (SUPPORTING)
• I really admire and respect your faith. (RESPECTING) Having faith is very important. (RESPECTING)
• Can you share with me what a miracle might look like for you? (EXPLORING)
	How much time do I have left?
	NOTE: This question may mean many things—they are scared, they want to know so they can plan, they are suffering, etc. Exploring what they want to know can be very helpful.
	• That is a great question. I am going to answer it the best that I can. Can you tell me what you are worried about? (EXPLORING)
	• That is a great question. I am going to answer it the best that I can. Can you tell me what information would be most helpful to you? (EXPLORING)
		Are you saying there is nothing more you can do?
		• I can't even imagine how (NAME EMOTION) this must be. (NAMING)
		• It sounds like you might be feeling ... (NAMING/EXPLORING)
		  a. Alone
		  b. Scared
		  c. Frustrated
		  d. Etc.
		• I wish we had a treatment that would cure you. Our team is here to help you through this. (SUPPORTING)

Are you telling me my dad is dying?
NOTE: These responses will affirm the question empathically—so do not use them if the patient is not dying.
• I wish I had better news. This must be such a shock for you. (NAMING)
• I can't even imagine how difficult this must be. (UNDERSTANDING)
	Are you giving up on me?
	• I wish we had more curative treatments to offer. Our team is committed to help you in every way we can. (SUPPORTING)
	• We will be here for you. (SUPPORTING)
	• It sounds like you might be feeling ... (NAMING/EXPLORING)
	  a. Alone
	  b. Scared
	  c. Etc.
	• We will work hard to get you the support that you need. (SUPPORTING)
		My dad is a fighter!
		• He is. He is such a strong person, and he has been through so much. (RESPECTING)
		• I admire that so much about him. (RESPECTING)
		• I really admire how much you care about your dad. (RESPECTING)
		• It must be (NAME EMOTION) to see him so sick. (NAMING)
		• Tell me more about your dad and what matters most to him. (EXPLORING)

Figure 12.2. Responses to Challenging Questions. Note: These phrases are examples of empathic continuers. Patients may not immediately respond to your first empathic statement. They will often need multiple successive empathic responses to their questions to work through an emotion. (Adapted from and made available for public use through a US Department of Veterans Affairs contract with VitalTalk, Order No. VA777-14-P-0400.)

You may be wondering, as some of my students were, "Are there any times that it's better to be sympathetic versus empathetic?" Robert Glazer, in his blog on September 9, 2021, writes that sympathy typically doesn't require a "corresponding emotion or understanding of a person's situation" and can therefore be more appropriate than empathy at "a distance, such as if you are offering condolences to someone outside your inner circle after they've lost a loved one. Sympathy can also be used to show respect for another person's situation, even if you do not relate to it personally."[23] Maybe this is best succinctly summarized in this quote from the author Rebecca O'Donnell: "Empathy is walking a mile in somebody else's moccasins. Sympathy is being sorry that their feet hurt."[24]

Cultivating Self-Empathy

When I meet with our PA students for their one-on-one EQ coaching session, the topic of self-empathy comes up, and the typical response of the student is "I'm harder on myself than others." Psychologist Donna Marino called this the "High Achievers Syndrome," recognizing that a syndrome is a constellation of signs and symptoms without any objective tests to diagnose it.[25] The *sine qua non* of the diagnosis is when you hear "I'm harder on myself than I am on others" or "I expect more of myself than others expect of themselves." High achievers tend to be their own harshest critics.

One student asked me how to be more forgiving to themselves. I asked how they would respond if a friend of theirs confided in them something personal like not doing well on a test or making a mistake on a patient. They responded that they would try to console them and encourage them to forgive themselves, reassure them that we are human, and we don't always do as well as we want. Try better next time. Learn from their mistakes. Do the best you can. I suggested giving themself the same advice and grace as one would give to another, although in fairness, it has taken me years to accept this lesson myself. Dr. Helen Reiss, a Harvard psychiatrist, teaches us the following in her book *The Empathy Effect*:

Self-empathy is not self-pity. Self-empathy is knowing that all human beings, including you, deserve understanding, compassion, forgiveness, and love even when you make mistakes that make you feel angry or embarrassed. It's an exercise in humility, in which you acknowledge that you are human and that mistakes are part of being human. It's an opportunity for learning and growth, though it doesn't relieve you of the responsibility of apologizing if you let someone down. Research has shown that people who practice self-empathy are more motivated and resilient, are more creative thinkers, and have greater life satisfaction and greater empathy toward others than those with less self-empathy who tend to have more hostility, anxiety, depression, and lower life satisfaction. Think of it this way. Self-empathy is the equivalent of oxygen masks on a plane. Before you can offer it to others, you need to put on your own mask first. Reiss reminds us that "As Alexander Pope wrote, 'To err is human.' But let's not forget the second part, 'To forgive, divine.'" And maybe most importantly, "The way we treat ourselves is often the way we treat others."[26]

Putting EQ into Action

Read the scenarios below and ask yourself the following questions: *In this example, what would I ideally want to be the outcome of the conversation and what would I want to avoid? How might my level of empathy be different if I was exhausted and/or being berated?*

   1. You are a clinician about to go into the exam room to explain to a patient that the reason they are doing so poorly with their medical condition is because of a significant error you made in managing their case. Before going into the room, you pause to consider what the different outcomes of the conversation may be.

2. You are a nurse working in the emergency department at the end of a long shift and after being in the ED for many days in a row. You are very tired, trying to "crawl to the finish line," get home, and have a few days off to rest and reload. However, one last patient comes in. He is a drunk driver who just hit another vehicle, causing significant injury to the other passengers. He is bleeding from a multitude of cuts on his face and torso and is in a lot of pain from other sustained injuries. He is begging for pain relief while also being abusive to you, calling you names and using obscenities.

3. You're a student on a clinical rotation seeing a woman in the emergency department exam room who looks battered, with many bruises and cuts and in obvious pain. She tells you that her husband did this to her . . . again.

Chapter Takeaways

1. Self-direction is knowing what you want and want to avoid, and making decisions in alignment with that. If you are making decisions that are not in alignment with that, you might not be making the right decisions for yourself. Making decisions in alignment with what you want and don't want will increase the likelihood of staying in your zone and keeping it wide.

2. Self-direction is knowing what gives you meaning and purpose, why it does, and pursuing it. It's also knowing what you want each day and with each interaction.

3. There are several exercises that you can use to assist you in discovering your why.

4. Empathy is a powerful connector of people, helping us feel *with* another. Connecting with people helps us all get through life a little easier and keeps us in our zone.

5. The elements of empathy parallel the elements of EQ: self- and social awareness, self- and relationship management, and self-direction.

6. The challenges of being empathic include recognizing the difference between sympathy and empathy, selective empathy, being empathic when you are suffering from compassion fatigue, self-empathy, and being empathic while navigating your emotions.

Conclusion

We define emotional intelligence as the subset of social intelligence that involves the ability to monitor one's own and others' feelings and emotions, to discriminate among them and to use this information to guide one's thinking and actions.

—SALOVEY AND MAYER

The premise of my book, and my *prescription* for you, is this: as a clinician, nurse, or future clinician or nurse, to *thrive in health care*, delivering the care that you want to deliver and your patients want to receive, you MUST manage and *put yourself first*. Though it may sound like heresy, patients come second. If you are not at your very best, it is very hard to give your best and for your patients to receive your best. How to be at your best to deliver your best, in real time, even when the heat is on and the stress is high? By using the Emotional Intelligence Zone structure and strategy.

Every time I walk through the hospital, I am reminded of health care's pain points. I hear it in the clinicians' and nurses' words and their tones of voice as I pass them in the halls and at the nurses' stations. I see it in their facial expressions and body language as they manage their challenging and sometimes demanding patients. I also see the stresses on the PA students in our program, who have little control over their time as they take a large number of course credits and endless exams proving their technical competence, and the toll it takes on many of them.

In health care, the expectations and stakes are always high, the time is short, and there is no room for error. When cases go well, there are few things in life as rewarding as making a diagnosis based upon a thorough history, physical exam, and appropriate imaging, cardiac tests, and lab data, then instituting the best treatment plan and seeing the patient respond favorably. On the other hand, there can be few lower moments in a clinician's and nurse's professional life than missing a diagnosis and seeing a patient, a person, a family, suffer. As clinicians and nurses, we can potentially go through these gyrations of highs and lows several times a day as we ride the daily health-care roller coaster.

Being in health care can be a very privileged position, affording the opportunity to help people during their most vulnerable times and making them better, though it comes with the high cost of stress, burnout, substance abuse, divorce, and suicide. We in health care have spent so much time, effort, energy, and money learning our skills. Don't we deserve to be able to enjoy our work, relish it, and to look forward to returning to work after a long weekend or a well-deserved vacation, instead of fretting about a return to the office, clinic, hospital, or classroom (the Sunday night syndrome), or barely surviving our practices, or considering retiring early, counting the days?

This book was intended to give you a structure and a strategy, the EQ Zone, to manage the inevitable challenges that come our way all day every day in the health-care profession. We have little control over many of these challenges. What *can* we control? Ourselves. We are emotional beings with an entire portion of our brain, the limbic system, dedicated to emotions that are constantly stimulated when functioning in the health-care arena. Emotions are data and can be wonderful allies when making decisions. Emotions also help connect us as human beings, person to person, in our personal and professional lives. The key is to be smarter with those emotions, and that is where the structure and strategy of the EQ Zone comes into play. Whether you are feeling up or down, high or low, good or bad, there is a place for the EQ Zone.

The benefits of being skilled with your EQ Zone are numerous, personally, and professionally: better decision-making, enhanced relationships, greater well-being, and improved quality of life, leading to enhanced job satisfaction, patient satisfaction and outcomes, reduced risk of malpractice, less chance of burnout, improved leadership skills, improved recruitment and retention of staff, and a better organizational culture and climate.

Since I became aware of the EQ Zone, I think about it and use it all day every day, and it works to get me through. To enhance my self-awareness, I check in with myself regularly. Am I in my zone or not? Is it wide or narrow? Am I in it or out? High or low? What am I thinking and what emotions am I feeling? Am I recognizing my patterns? Have I been in a similar situation before, and how did I handle it? Is there something I could and should do differently this time that would make for a better outcome?

I also try to be socially aware, "reading the room." Is the person or people I am interacting with in their zone(s) or not? What are they thinking and feeling? Am I paying close attention to their nonverbal communications as much as what they are saying, and are they consistent? Do I appreciate their brain preferences and recognize that they might not be the same as mine, and adjust accordingly? Am I cognizant of the timing of what to do and say and when to do and say it?

Once it's time to act, am I intentional with my decisions using logic, emotions, intrinsic motivation, and optimism to make my best decisions, recognizing that these decisions, given the choices I have, can positively or negatively impact the outcome and my reputation? If my zone is narrow or I am bumped out of it, what strategies do I have at my disposal to widen my zone or get back into it? I use strategies like "name it to tame it," saying to myself, "Man, my zone is narrow now" or "I am out of my zone." It clues me in to hit the pause button, allowing me to respond instead of reacting. By pausing, I can be extra cautious in how I respond, rather than merely reacting, since I am more apt to do or say something that might bring heartache when I react. I also have other strategies at my disposal to help me get back in my zone if I do get bumped out, like deep box breathing, grounding, resourcing, and even a few F-bombs or M-Fs (quietly under my breath, of course). It's good to know that different people prefer different strategies to get them back in their zones, and what works for some might not work for others.

When I am involved in a conversation, with hopes of developing and maintaining relationships, I make the conscious decision to be a generous, loud listener, listening with my ears and eyes and doing so with curiosity and without judgment, seeking to understand by listening for intent, content, and emotions. People prefer to talk with a good listener rather than a good speaker. When it's finally my turn to speak, I try to say the right thing at the right time to the right person with the right tone of voice. Whenever possible I "VET" the conversation: **V**alidating, **E**xploring, and **T**ransforming the person's story or situation rather than one-upping them with mine. When the opportunity presents itself, I welcome hearing other people's stories, noting that what ultimately connects us are our stories and empathy. I also try to overcome the challenges of empathy, such as being selective, being empathic when I'm exhausted, wallowing in another person's misfortune, and resisting the self-empathy that allows myself grace and forgiveness when I make inevitable mistakes.

Lastly, I try never to lose sight or consciousness of what truly gives me meaning and purpose, and why, and what I want each day. With each conversation and interaction, I try to consider what emotional wake I want to leave behind for myself and the organization I am representing. If you are making decisions that are not in alignment with what you want and don't want, you might be making the wrong decisions for yourself.

I admit that executing all this consistently, perfectly, is challenging and practically unachievable. However, with practice, given that emotional intelligence is a learnable competency, augmented by one knowing their own EQ strengths and opportunities by completing an EQ assessment, we can all get better at it. And, given the brain's ability for neuroplasticity, the more we practice emotional intelligence, the more we become emotionally intelligent. Imagine what the world would look like if we were all a little bit more emotionally intelligent.

I greatly appreciate you reading this book to its conclusion. As my Venezuelan hematology professor used to say, with his very strong accent, way back when I was in medical school, "You make an old man happy." That old man today is me. What would make me most happy is having more clinicians, nurses, and clinician/nursing students use the EQ Zone, which I believe would translate into you being your best; being well; enjoying your chosen profession; being less likely to burn out, leave your field prematurely, or suffer a malpractice case; and more frequently delivering (even) better patient care. And since we are all human and have lives outside of work as well, we would transfer these skills to our personal lives, hopefully making the world more peaceful and harmonious, one person and interaction at a time. Just as the journey of a thousand miles begins with the first step, the journey to making health care and the world better begins with the individual, and that person, now that you are familiar with the EQ Zone, is you.

I fully recognize that change is difficult. Albert Einstein is believed to have said, "The measure of intelligence is the ability to change."[1] I submit there are fewer people that are smarter than those in health care. I'd feel very satisfied if even just one person reading this book was able to make that change. Helping one helps many, given the large number of patients that clinicians and nurses interact with daily.

I'll end with a quote from one of the godfathers of Emotional Intelligence, Daniel Goleman, from his book *Emotional Intelligence: Why It Can Matter More Than IQ*: "People high on the EQ chart tend to be masters of both work and play. They usually have prosperous careers, long lasting, fulfilling relationships, and tons of friends. They are often generous, empathic, self-motivated, with the ability to love and be loved."[2]

Now you know how to be that person.

But wait, there is more. If you would like to put all that you have learned during the reading of this book to your own personal test (no passing or failing), then please move on to the Appendix, where I offer you a variety of cases that give you the opportunity to practice using the zone and all the EQ components together.

Acknowledgments

I'd like to thank my wife, Anne Ruffer, for her never-ending, unwavering, and unconditional love and support for this book and all my other projects.

I am eternally grateful and indebted to Drs. Mary Jumbelic, Janet Mark, Jef Sneider, Bob Weisenthal, Jeny Paterson, and Professor Beth Mercer for taking their precious time, energy, wisdom, caring, and kindness to read through my manuscript, especially the earlier versions. Their insightful, thoughtful, constructive, and productive feedback helped to shape my book for the better, making it more meaningful and valuable to the future readers.

I'd like to recognize Drs. Barbara Davis, Peter Hatherley-Greene, and Bill Holmes for sharing their expert editing skills with me, taking a raw writing of the manuscript and helping to make it much more organized and readable during the early phases of the book. I'd also like to give a shout-out to my new friends at Greenleaf Book Group (GBG), including editors Lessie Schrider, Karen Cakebread, Melinda Andrews, and lead editor Tess Newton, a godsend and guardian angel, who, with their editing and guidance, helped transform the book into its final version. I also appreciate Jenny Cribb for helping to develop a business integration action plan for the book assisting me to disseminate EQ to clinicians, nurses, and students and to Neil Gonzalez for his skills and efficiency to design the interior and cover of the book, Benito Salazar for overseeing the book project, and Justin Branch for helping me begin my journey with GBG. Thank you also to Brittany Jones-Pugh, Gwen Cunningham, Guy Muller, Kyle Pearson, Matthew MacMillan, and Cody Bentley. Certainly, with the help, guidance, and support of GBG, my book, a pure labor of love for my health-care profession and the people that we serve, has come to fruition, helping to educate all in health care on the benefits and value of EQ professionally and personally.

Since 2018, Six Seconds has contributed mightily to the start and progression of my understanding of the benefits of emotional intelligence. Hala Jimenez has been a wonderful facilitator, helping me communicate and connect with all areas of Six Seconds. President and CEO of Six Seconds Josh Freedman is an amazing human being, worthy of a role model, for how he took his idea of educating and researching EQ and grew it into a multinational organization with the goal of making the world a more peaceful and harmonious place to live. He deserves all my respect and gratitude.

I am grateful to Drs. Britt Berrett, Michael Roscoe, and Seth Kronenberg, and Paul Spiegelman and Lynne Shopiro for taking their valuable and limited time to read through my book prior to its release and find the book worthy of their generous endorsements. Thank you!!

Lastly, I am constantly inspired and motivated by my parents, Nat and Gloria Lebowitz; my brother, Jay Lebowitz, and his wife, Maryanne; my in-laws Lowell and Ruth Ruffer, Susan Ruffer, Jim Ruffer, and Galya Ben Arieh Ruffer; all my nieces and nephews; my children, Rachel Bycer and Sam Lebowitz; their spouses, Efrem Bycer and Jess Liban; and my three amazing granddaughters, Shayna, Becca, and Talia. Their love and support buoys me up to be the best version of myself that I can possibly be and to make the world a better place for them, and all, to live in.

Putting It All Together: Using the EQ Zone to Manage Health-Care Pain Points

We cannot tell what may happen to us in the strange medley of life.
But we can decide what happens in us—how we can take it,
what we do with it—and that is what really counts in the end.

—JOSEPH FORT NEWTON

I'd like to introduce you to another Six Seconds concept called the "reaction cycle."[1]

The reaction cycle is a succinct visual overview of the EQ Zone. The "setup" is the zone you are in at a particular moment. If your setup zone is wide and you are feeling your best self and then get "triggered," you might interpret the trigger differently than if your zone were narrow. Your "reaction" might also be more constructive and productive with a

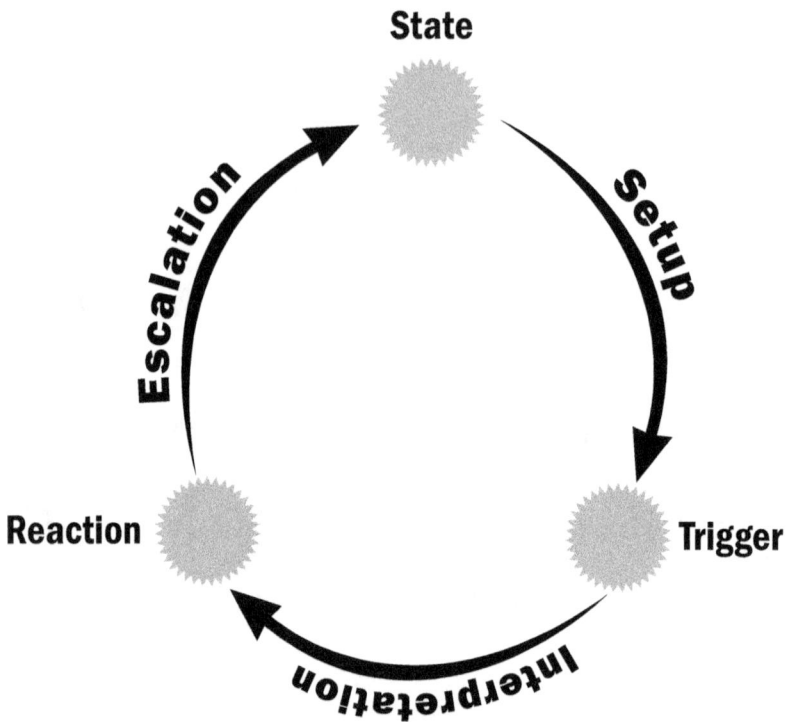

Figure A.1. The reaction cycle. (Reproduced with permission from Six Seconds.)

wide zone, and the situation would more likely de-escalate than escalate. However, if your setup zone was narrow and the same trigger occurred, your interpretation and reaction to the trigger might escalate the situation, bumping you out of your zone and potentially going down a path of no return, causing regrets or remorse.

Throughout this book there were case presentations at the end of each chapter, with the intent of identifying and educating on the different components of the zone and emotional intelligence. The remainder of this section is to give you the opportunity to put all the EQ components together to help you go from theory to practice. Here are the instructions.

Picture what zone, the setup, you might have been in before each of the following scenarios arose. How might you respond differently if your zone was wide or narrow before the scenario arose, or even if you were bumped out of your zone before this all happened?

1. How might this trigger impact your interpretation or change your zone?

2. Can you identify/recognize, name, and interpret what you feel in this situation and understand where this feeling is coming from (self-awareness/emotional literacy)?

3. Can you recall any similar situations in your past, including how you handled it and the outcome (self-awareness/recognizing patterns)?

4. Do you have a sense for what that other person in this scenario might be thinking and feeling and what zone they might be in? Also consider how their response might change, depending on if their zone was wide or narrow or if they were bumped out of their zone (social awareness)?

5. How might you manage/interpret this scenario? React or pause and respond? What would you do and say (self-management)?

6. How can you tell if your response was favorable to your relationship with this person or not? That is, they picked up what you put down and you picked up what they put down (relationship management).

7. What was your level of empathy during this situation, for the other person and yourself?

8. Did your response escalate or de-escalate the situation?

9. What did you really want and not want at the end of this scenario? Did you achieve what you desired? Did you end up in the state you wanted?

Below are twenty scenarios that hopefully are representative of real life. Feel free to work on just the ones that resonate most with you. Also, please consider adding your own scenarios that you might have experienced in the past and put them through this exercise to see if you would feel, think, do, say, or want something different than what ended up happening before. If you're ready, please begin.

Scenario 1: You're a clinician in a group practice and one of your partners is going out for six months on maternity leave. You are already working longer hours and seeing more patients than you prefer, though now you are being asked to do more covering for your partner.

You're a nurse already responsible for more patients than you think is safe and feeling exhausted trying to keep up, when one of your nurse colleagues suddenly has to take a medical leave of absence. Your supervisor asks you to be a "team player" and step up to do more shifts and hours.

You're a student in a health-care education program running on near empty using every minute of your waking day, even sacrificing sleep, studying just to keep up and pass your exams, when one of your classmates has a family emergency and needs to take time away from the class. They ask you if you can keep them current on the topics being taught and call them each night to do so.

Scenario 2: Your patient gave you a compliment for all the good care you've given them and followed it up with a gift.

Scenario 3: A patient confronted you about a perceived mistake you made in their care that caused them harm.

Scenario 4: You're with a large group of people on hospital rounds and one of the attendees says something sarcastic/derogatory to you in front of everyone else.

Scenario 5: You are at a party having a good, relaxed time, and someone finds out you're in health care. They begin asking you questions about their care and what they should do.

Scenario 6: A new patient begins telling you about a previous clinician or nurse who had a terrible bedside manner and/or made errors in their care.

Scenario 7: A patient comes back to your office after seeing another clinician who had an opinion different from yours.

Scenario 8: Your patient makes a derogatory comment about religion, or sexual identity or preference, not knowing that was your religion, or sexual identity or preference.

Scenario 9: You're a clinician or a nurse working in a big health-care system. You were promised a bonus and a raise at the end of the fiscal year, but now the financial officer sends you an email saying that, in retrospect, you didn't meet the criteria to merit the raise or bonus that you had expected.

Scenario 10: You witness a colleague (clinician, nurse, or student) give great care to a patient.

Scenario 11: A patient comes on to you sexually in the office.

Scenario 12: A patient calls you by your first name without inquiring how you would like to be addressed.

Scenario 13: You're in a health-care education program when the patient you are seeing refuses to talk with you and only wants to see the "real" doctor or nurse.

Scenario 14: A patient calls the leadership of the organization you are working for and complains that you touched them inappropriately and they want you to face some consequences. You don't recall that you did anything inappropriately.

Scenario 15: You are served malpractice papers from a patient to whom you gave a lot of extra energy, effort, and time trying to improve their medical condition.

Scenario 16: You're a female clinician and the patient calls you "honey" or "sweetie" or "nurse."

Scenario 17: A colleague of yours gets and takes credit from someone else for doing something great when you were really the one that did so.

Scenario 18: A patient or colleague is telling you about a great trip they took or a great feat they accomplished. You actually had a similar trip or had an even greater feat than theirs.

Scenario 19: You had a bad day and your spouse or significant other or friend asks, "How was your day?"

Scenario 20: You're a health-care student, or nurse, or clinician, and you just took an exam and didn't do well, maybe even failed. Someone asks you how you did and whether you passed.

My hope is that this exercise gave you some additional insights and wisdom, helping you to advance your own emotional intelligence, and allowing you to stay in your zone and keep it wide more often. Please consider thinking about and using this reaction cycle strategy along with the emotional intelligence zone when the inevitable and inescapable real-life challenging situations find you in both your professional and personal lives. If you are able to navigate them better than you might have before reading this book, then you will have made an old man (me) happy, again.

Notes

Introduction

1. Moïra Mikolajczak, "The Impact of Emotional Intelligence on Physical Health," *Personality and Individual Differences* 60 (2014): S22, https://www.researchgate.net/publication/277530990_The_impact_of_emotional_intelligence_on_physical_health.

2. Jon McKenna, "Medscape Physician Burnout & Depression Report 2024: We Have Much Work to Do" (2024), https://www.medscape.com/slideshow/2024-lifestyle-burnout-6016865#8.

3. Sara Berg, "Burnout Benchmark: 28% Unhappy with Current Health Care Job," American Medical Association, May 17, 2022, accessed July 24, 2023, https://www.ama-assn.org/practice-management/physician-health/burnout-benchmark-28-unhappy-current-health-care-job; Tait D. Shanafelt, Colin P. West, Lotte N. Dyrbye, Mickey Trockel, Michael Tutty, Hanhan Wang, Lindsey E. Carlasare, and Christine Sinsky, "Changes in Burnout and Satisfaction with Work-Life Integration in Physicians During the First 2 Years of the COVID-19 Pandemic," *Mayo Clinic Proceedings* 97, no. 12 (2022): 2248–2258, doi:10.1016/j.mayocp.2022.09.002.

4. Jon McKenna, "Medscape Physician Burnout & Depression Report."

5. Jon McKenna, "Medscape Physician Burnout & Depression Report."

6. Jessica G. Rainbow, Katherine M. Dudding, Claire Bethel, Angie Norton, Christine Platt, Pankaj K. Vyas, and Maribeth Slebodnik, "Work-Related Health Conditions Among American Nurses: A Scoping Review," *SAGE Open Nursing* 10 (2024): 23779608241257026.

7. Jessica G. Rainbow et al., "Work-Related Health Conditions."

8. Radhika Chalasani, "Yogi Berra's Greatest Quotes," *CBS News*, May 12, 2015, https://www.cbsnews.com/pictures/yogi-berras-greatest-quotes-quips/.

9. "The Emotional Intelligence Network," Six Seconds, 2024, https://www.6seconds.org/

10. Mickey Lebowitz, *Losing My Patience: Why I Quit the Medical Game* (Gegensatz Press, 2009).

11. Britt Berrett and Paul Spiegelman, *Patients Come Second: Leading Change by Changing the Way You Lead* (An Inc Original, 2013).

Chapter 1

1. Elaine Miller-Karas, *Building Resilience to Trauma: The Trauma and Community Resiliency Models*, 2nd ed. (Routledge, 2023).

2. Mihaly Csikszentmihalyi, *Flow: The Psychology of Optimal Experience*, 1st ed. (Harper Perennial Modern Classics, 2008).

3. Susan Scott, *Fierce Conversations: Achieving Success at Work and in Life, One Conversation at a Time* (Berkley Books, 2002).

4. Stephen Covey, *The 7 Habits of Highly Effective People* (Free Press, 1989).

5. Susan Scott, *Fierce Conversations*.

6. Alaa Abd-Elsayed, Adam Rupp, Ryan S. D'Souza, Nasir Hussain, Adam J. Milam, Natalie Strand, Omar Viswanath, Steven Falowski, Dawood Sayed, and Timothy Deer, "Interventional Pain Physician Burnout During the COVID-19 Pandemic: A Survey from the American Society of Pain and Neuroscience," *Current Pain and Headache Reports* 27, no. 8 (2023): 259–267, doi:10.1007/s11916-023-01121-6.

7. Christina Maslach and Michael P. Leiter, "Understanding the Burnout Experience: Recent Research and Its Implications for Psychiatry," *World Psychiatry* 15, no. 2 (2016): 103–111.

8. Shirzad Chamine, *Positive Intelligence: Why Only 20% of Teams and Individuals Achieve Their True Potential and How You Can Achieve Yours* (Greenleaf Book Group Press, 2012).

Chapter 2

1. Michael Vallejo, "Emotions vs. Feelings vs. Moods," Mental Health Center Kids, December 1, 2023, accessed June 10, 2024, https://mentalhealthcenterkids.com/blogs/articles/emotions-vs-feelings-vs-moods.

2. Fushun Wang, Jiongjiong Yang, Fang Pan, Roger C. Ho, and Jason H. Huang, "Neurotransmitters and Emotions," *Frontiers in Psychology* 11 (2020): 21.

3. Peter Salovey and John D. Mayer, "Emotional Intelligence," *Imagination, Cognition and Personality* 9, no. 3 (1990): 185–211.

4. Susan Scott, *Fierce Conversations*, 5.

5. Mark Collier, "Hume's Theory of Moral Imagination," *History of Philosophy Quarterly* 27, no. 3 (2010): 255–273, https://www.jstor.org/stable/27809509.

6. Remy Debes, "From Einfühlung to Empathy: Sympathy in Early Phenomenology and Psychology," *Oxford Academic* (2015): 286–322, https://doi.org/10.1093/acprof:oso/9780199928873.003.0015.

7. Mark Collier, "Hume's Theory of Moral Imagination."

8. Remy Debes, "From Einfühlung to Empathy."

9. Daisy Grewal and Peter Salovey, "Feeling Smart: The Science of Emotional Intelligence," American Scientist, 2005, https://www.americanscientist.org/article/feeling-smart-the-science-of-emotional-intelligence.

10. Daniel Goleman, *Emotional Intelligence: Why It Can Matter More Than IQ* (Bantam, 1995), https://www.amazon.ae/Emotional-Intelligence-Matter-More-Than/dp/055338371X.

11. "What Is BlueEQ?," BlueEQ, March 2024, https://blueeq.com/.

12. Travis Bradberry and Jean Greaves, *Emotional Intelligence 2.0* (TalentSmart, 2009), 24.

13. "The Six Seconds Model of EQ," Six Seconds, 2024, https://www.6seconds.org/2010/01/27/the-six-seconds-eq-model/.

14. Jonah Lehrer, *How We Decide* (Houghton Mifflin, 2009).

15. "Self-Awareness Starts Here," The Myers-Briggs Company, accessed June 10, 2024, https://www.themyersbriggs.com/MBTI.

16. Annabelle Lim, "Big Five Personality Traits: The 5-Factor Model of Personality," Simply Psychology, December 20, 2023, accessed June 10, 2024, https://www.simplypsychology.org/big-five-personality.html.

17. "What Is Emotional Intelligence?," Universal Class, accessed June 10, 2024, https://www.universalclass.com/articles/psychology/emotional-intelligence/what-is-emotional-intelligence.htm.

18. Christopher Soto and Oliver P. John, "Development of Big Five Domains and Facets in Adulthood: Mean-Level Age Trends and Broadly Versus Narrowly Acting Mechanisms," *Journal of Personality* 80, no. 4 (2012): 881–914, doi: 10.1111/j.1467-6494.2011.00752.x.

19. Neha Taneja, Sujata Gupta, Vinoth Gnana Chellaiyan, Aanchal Anant Awasthi, and Sandeep Sachdeva, "Personality Traits as a Predictor of Emotional Intelligence Among Medical Students," *Journal of Education and Health Promotion* 9, no. 1 (2020): 354, doi: 10.4103/jehp.jehp_678_19. PMID: 33575390.

20. "10 Ways Manipulators Use Emotional Intelligence for Evil (and How to Fight Back)," *Inc.*, August 23, 2016, https://www.inc.com/justin-bariso/10-ways-manipulators-use-emotional-intelligence-for-evil-and-how-to-fight-back.html.

21. "The Dark Side of Emotional Intelligence: Are You Being Manipulated?," Medium, August 10, 2023, https://medium.com/@terrayou/the-dark-side-of-emotional-intelligence-are-you-being-manipulated-c66586277d32.

Chapter 3

1. "What Is BlueEQ?," BlueEQ, March 2024, https://blueeq.com/.

2. Travis Bradberry and Jean Greaves, *Emotional Intelligence 2.0* (TalentSmart, 2009).

3. "The Six Seconds Model of EQ."

4. "State of the Heart: 2024 Report," Six Seconds, https://www.6seconds.org/emotional-intelligence/research/.

5. Ashley Thompson and Daniel Voyer, "Sex Differences in the Ability to Recognise Non-Verbal Displays of Emotion: A Meta-Analysis," *Cognition and Emotion* 28, no. 7 (2014): 1164–1195, doi:10.1080/02699931.2013.875889; Leonardo Christov-Moore, Elizabeth A.

Simpson, Gino Coudé, Kristina Grigaityte, Marco Iacoboni, and Pier Francesco Ferrari, "Empathy: Gender Effects in Brain and Behavior," *Neuroscience & Biobehavioral Reviews* 46 (2014): 604–627, doi:10.1016/j. neubiorev.2014.09.001; Mariska Kret and Beatrice De Gelder, "A Review on Sex Differences in Processing Emotional Signals," *Neuropsychologia* 50, no. 7 (2012): 1211–1221, doi:10.1016/j.neuropsychologia. 2011.12.022.

6. "Which Generation Is Most Emotionally Intelligent?," Six Seconds, 2018, https://www.6seconds.org/2018/11/15/best-generation-for-eq/.

Chapter 4

1. Sandra Hockenbury, Susan Nolan, and Don Hockenbury, *Discovering Psychology, Seventh Edition* (Worth Publishers, January 1, 2016).

2. Daniel Goleman, *Emotional Intelligence*.

3. Joseph Ledoux, *The Emotional Brain: The Mysterious Underpinnings of Emotional Life* (Simon and Schuster, 1998).

4. Norman Schmidt, Anthony Richey, Michael Zvolensky, and Jon Maner, "Exploring Human Freeze Responses to a Threat Stressor," *Journal of Behavior Therapy and Experimental Psychiatry* 39, no. 3 (2008): 292-304, https://www.ncbi.nlm.nih.gov/pmc/articles/PMC2489204/.

5. Daniel Siegel and Tina Bryson, *The Whole-Brain Child* (Delacorte Press, 2011).

6. Gregor Hasler, Stephen Fromm, Ruben P. Alvarez, David A. Luckenbaugh, Wayne C. Drevets, and Christian Grillon, "Cerebral Blood Flow in Immediate and Sustained Anxiety," *Journal of Neuroscience* 27, no. 23 (2007): 6313–6319, doi:10.1523/JNEUROSCI.5369-06.2007.

7. Mary Nord Cook, "Chapter 4—PACK-Teen Treatment Protocol," in *Transforming Teen Behavior* (Academic Press, 2015): 27–162, https://doi. org/10.1016/B978-0-12-803357-9.00004-0; Andrea Gold, Lisa Marie Shin, S. P. Orr, M. A. Carson, S. L. Rauch, M. L. Macklin, N. B. Lasko, et al., "Decreased Regional Cerebral Blood Flow in Medial Prefrontal Cortex During Trauma-Unrelated Stressful Imagery in Vietnam Veterans with Post-Traumatic Stress Disorder," *Psychological Medicine* 41, no. 12 (2011): 2563–2572.

8. Amy Arnsten, "Stress Signalling Pathways That Impair Prefrontal Cortex Structure and Function," *Nature Reviews Neuroscience* 10, no. 6 (2009): 410–422, doi:10.1038/nrn2648.

9. E. C. McCanlies, M. Leppma, A. Mnatsakanova, P. Allison, D. Fekedulegn, M. E. Andrew, and J. M. Violanti, "Associations of Burnout with Awakening and Diurnal Cortisol Among Police Officers," *Comprehensive Psychoneuroendocrinology* 4 (2020): 100016, doi: 10.1016/j.cpnec.2020.100016.

10. Vagisha Sharma, Manpreet Kaur, Supriya Gupta, and Raj Kapoor, "Relationship of Emotional Intelligence, Intelligence Quotient, and Autonomic Reactivity Tests in Undergraduate Medical Students," *Medical Science Educator* 29 (2019): 673–681, doi:10.1007/s40670-019-00763-9.

11. Joshua Freedman, "12 Practical Tips for Emotional Wellbeing by Being Smarter with Feelings," Six Seconds, 2023, accessed June 5, 2024, https://www.6seconds.org/2023/06/19/tips-for-emotional-wellbeing/.

12. Britta K. Hölzel, James Carmody, Mark Vangel, Christina Congleton, Sita M. Yerramsetti, Tim Gard, and Sara W. Lazar, "Mindfulness Practice Leads to Increases in Regional Brain Gray Matter Density," *Psychiatry Research: Neuroimaging* 191, no. 1 (2011): 36–43.

13. Tammi Kral, Brianna S. Schuyler, Jeanette A. Mumford, Melissa A. Rosenkranz, Antoine Lutz, and Richard J. Davidson, "Impact of Short- and Long-Term Mindfulness Meditation Training on Amygdala Reactivity to Emotional Stimuli," *Neuroimage* 181 (2018): 301–313.

14. Jodi Schulz, "Emotions Are Contagious: Learn What Science and Research Has to Say About It," Michigan State University, 2017, accessed June 5, 2024, https://www.canr.msu.edu/news/emotions_are_contagious_learn_what_science_and_research_has_to_say_about_it.

15. Nicholas Christakis and James Fowler, *Connected: The Surprising Power of Our Social Networks and How They Shape Our Lives* (Little, Brown, 2009).

16. Ray Williams, "How Your Mood—Good or Bad—Can Be Contagious," LinkedIn, January 10, 2024, accessed June 5, 2024, https://www.linkedin.com/pulse/how-your-mood-good-bad-can-contagious-ray-williams-amjuc/.

17. Giuseppe di Pellegrino, Luciano Fadiga, Leonardo Fogassi, Vittorio Gallese, and Giacomo Rizzolatti, "Understanding Motor Events: A Neurophysiological Study," *Experimental Brain Research* 91 (1992): 176–180, doi:10.1007/BF00230027.

Chapter 5

1. Gregory Feist and Frank Barton, "Emotional Intelligence and Academic Intelligence in Career and Life Success: Paper Presented to the Annual Convention of the American Psychological Society," San Francisco, CA, June (1996).

2. Hui-Ching Weng, Chao-Ming Hung, Yi-Tien Liu, Yu-Jen Cheng, Cheng-Yo Yen, Chi-Chang Chang, and Chih-Kun Huang, "Associations Between Emotional Intelligence and Doctor Burnout, Job Satisfaction and Patient Satisfaction," *Medical Education* 45, no. 8 (2011): 835–842.

3. Keith Cavaness, Anthony Picchioni, and James W. Fleshman, "Linking Emotional Intelligence to Successful Health Care Leadership: The Big Five Model of Personality," *Clinics in Colon and Rectal Surgery* 33, no. 4 (2020): 195–203.

4. Barbara Rebecca Mutonyi, Terje Slåtten, and Gudbrand Lien, "Organizational Climate and Creative Performance in the Public Sector," *European Business Review* 32, no. 4 (2020): 615–631, https://www.emerald.com/insight/content/doi/10.1108/EBR-02-2019-0021/full/html.

5. Ingrid M. Nembhard, Guy David, Iman Ezzeddine, David Betts, and Jennifer Radin, "A Systematic Review of Research on Empathy in Health Care," *Health Services Research* 58, no. 2 (2023): 250–263.

6. "White Paper: Emotional Intelligence and Success," Six Seconds, accessed June 10, 2024, https://www.6seconds.org/2019/03/12/white-paper-emotional-intelligence-and-success/.

7. Travis Bradberry and Jean Greaves, *Emotional Intelligence 2.0.* (TalentSmart, 2009)

8. Travis Bradberry, *Self-Awareness: The Hidden Driver of Success and Satisfaction* (Pedigree Trade, 2009).

9. Naim El-Aswad, Zeina Ghossoub, and Relly Nadler, *Physician Burnout: An Emotionally Malignant Disease* (North Charleston, SC: Create Space Publishing, 2017).

10. "Physician Lifestyle & Happiness Report," Medscape, 2023, accessed June 2024, https://www.medscape.com/sites/public/lifestyle/2023.

11. Tait D. Shanafelt, Colin P. West, Lotte N. Dyrbye, Mickey Trockel, Michael Tutty, Hanhan Wang, Lindsey E. Carlasare, and Christine Sinsky, "Changes in Burnout and Satisfaction with Work-Life Integration in Physicians During the First 2 Years of the COVID-19 Pandemic," *Mayo Clinic Proceedings* 97, no. 12 (2022), https://doi.org/10.1016/j.mayocp.2022.09.002. Accessed June 10, 2024.

12. "2022 Physician Report: Most Physicians Would Not Recommend a Medical Career to Their Child," Medical Economics, June 17, 2022, accessed June 10, 2024, https://www.medicaleconomics.com/view/2022-physician-report-most-physicians-would-not-recommend-a-medical-career-to-their-child.

13. Ron Southwick, "Many Nurses Aren't Just Unhappy with Their Jobs. They're Losing the Love of Nursing," Chief Healthcare Executive, August 23, 2022, accessed June 10, 2025, https://www.chiefhealthcareexecutive.com/view/many-nurses-aren-t-just-unhappy-with-their-jobs-they-re-losing-the-love-of-nursing-.

14. Barnabas Nwankwo, Tobias C. Obi, Ngozi Sydney-Agbor, Soloman A. Agu, and James U. Aboh, "Relationship Between Emotional Intelligence and Job Satisfaction Among Health Workers," *IOSR Journal of Nursing and Health Science* 2, no. 5 (2013): 19–23, https://www.researchgate.net/publication/378881721_Relationship_Between_Emotional_Intelligence_And_Job_Satisfaction_among_Health_Workers.

15. James Parker, Laura J. Summerfeldt, Catherine Walmsley, Ryan O'Byrne, Hiten P. Dave, and A. Geoffrey Crane, "Trait Emotional Intelligence and Interpersonal Relationships: Results from a 15-year Longitudinal Study," *Personality and Individual Differences* 169 (2021): 110013, doi:10.1016/j.paid.2020.110013.

16. Panagiotis V. Polychroniou, "Relationship Between Emotional Intelligence and Transformational Leadership of Supervisors: The Impact on Team Effectiveness," *Team Performance Management: An International Journal* 15, no. 7/8 (2009): 343–356, doi:10.1108/13527590911002122.

17. Saras Ramesar, Pieter Koortzen, and Rudolf M. Oosthuizen, "The Relationship Between Emotional Intelligence and Stress Management," *SA Journal of Industrial Psychology* 35, no. 1 (2009): 39–48, doi:10.4102/sajip.v35i1.443.

18. Flora Ioannidou and Vaya Konstantikaki, "Empathy and Emotional Intelligence: What Is It Really About?," *International Journal of Caring Siences* 1, no. 3 (2008): 118.

19. M. Afzalur Rahim, Clement Psenicka, Panagiotis Polychroniou, Jing-Hua Zhao, Chun-Sheng Yu, Kawai Anita Chan, Kwok Wai Yee Susana, Maria G. Alves, Chang-Won Lee, Sahidur Ralunan, Shameema Ferdausy, and Rene van Wyk, "A Model of Emotional Intelligence and Conflict Management Strategies: A Study in Seven Countries," *The International Journal of Organizational Analysis* 10, no. 4 (2002): 302–326.

20. Anupam B. Jena, Seth Seabury, Darius Lakdawalla, and Amitabh Chandra, "Malpractice Risk According to Physician Specialty," *New England Journal of Medicine* 365, no. 7 (2011): 629–636, doi:10.1056/NEJMsa1012370.

21. Nichole Bazemore, "Does Your Doctor Have Malpractice Claims? How to Find Out," *Forbes*, April 19, 2016, accessed June 10, 2024, https://www.forbes.com/sites/amino/2016/04/19/does-your-doctor-have-malpractice-claims-how-to-find-out/?sh=6c4f31f55a64.

22. "2024 Medical Malpractice Statistics," Miller & Zois, LLC, accessed June 10, 2024, https://www.millerandzois.com/medical-malpractice/medical-malpractice statistics/.

23. A. Gallegos, "Medscape Malpractice Report 2023: Is Your Risk of Being Sued Climbing?," Medscape, October 26, 2023, accessed June 10, 2024, https://www.medscape.com/slideshow/2023-malpractice-report-6016734#4.

24. Daniel Shouhed, Catherine Beni, Nicholas Manguso, Waguih William IsHak, and Bruce L. Gewertz, "Association of Emotional Intelligence with Malpractice Claims: A Review," *JAMA Surgery* 154, no. 3 (2019): 250–256, doi:10.1001/jamasurg.2018.5065.

25. Daniel Shouhed et al., "Association of Emotional Intelligence."

26. J. McKenna, "Medscape Endocrinologist Burnout & Depression Report 2024," Medscape, March 29, 2024, accessed June 10, 2024, https://www.medscape.com/slideshow/2024-burnout-endocrinologist-6016971.

27. David A. Hyman, Joshua Lerner, David J. Magid, and Bernard Black, "Association of Past and Future Paid Medical Malpractice Claims," in *JAMA Health Forum*, vol. 4, no. 2 (2023): 225436–225436, doi:10.1001/jamahealthforum.2022.5436.

28. Razia Khammissa, Simon Nemutandani, Gal Feller, Johan Lemmer, and Liviu Feller, "Burnout Phenomenon: Neurophysiological Factors, Clinical Features, and Aspects of Management," *Journal of International Medical Research* 50, no. 9 (2022): 03000605221106428, doi:10.1177/03000605221106428.

29. Zhun Gong, Yuqi Chen, and Yayu Wang, "The Influence of Emotional Intelligence on Job Burnout and Job Performance: Mediating Effect of Psychological Capital," *Frontiers in Psychology* 10 (2019): 486722, doi:10.3389/fpsyg.2019.02707.

30. Yinyin Cao, Lei Gao, Lihua Fan, Mingli Jiao, Ye Li, and Yuanshuo Ma, "The Influence of Emotional Intelligence on Job Burnout of Healthcare Workers and Mediating Role of Workplace Violence: A Cross Sectional Study," *Frontiers in Public Health* 10 (2022): 892421, doi:10.3389/fpubh.2022.892421.

31. Kostantinos V. Petrides and Adrian Furnham, "Trait Emotional Intelligence: Behavioural Validation in Two Studies of Emotion Recognition and Reactivity to Mood Induction," *European Journal of Personality* 17, no. 1 (2003): 39–57.

32. Louise B. Andrew, "Physician Suicide," Medscape, July 13, 2022, https://emedicine.medscape.com/article/806779-overview?form=fpf.

33. Stewart Gandolf, "Good Doctor vs. Bad Doctor: How Patients Judge Provider Quality," Healthcare Success, 2023, https://healthcaresuccess.com/blog/doctor-marketing/good-doctor-vs-bad-doctor-patients-judge-provider-quality.html.

34. "Quote Origin: They May Forget What You Said, But They Will Never Forget How You Made Them Feel," Quote Investigator, April 6, 2014, https://quoteinvestigator.com/2014/04/06/they-feel/?amp=1.

35. Elmira Khademi, Mohammad Abdi, Mohammad Saeidi, Shahram Piri, and Robab Mohammadian, "Emotional Intelligence and Quality of Nursing Care: A Need for Continuous Professional Development," *Iranian Journal of Nursing and Midwifery Research* 26, no. 4 (2021): 361–367.

36. Gülay Oyur Celik, "The Relationship Between Patient Satisfaction and Emotional Intelligence Skills of Nurses Working in Surgical Clinics," *Patient Preference and Adherence* (2017): 1363–1368.

37. Abraham Zaleznik, "The 'Hawthorne Effect': What Mayo Urged in Broad Outline Has Become Part of the Orthodoxy of Modern Management," *Harvard Business School Historical Collections* (Baker Library, 1984), https://www.library.hbs.edu/hc/hawthorne/09.html.

38. Britt Berrett and Paul Spiegelman, *Patients Come Second*.

39. Peter McDonald, *Oxford Dictionary of Medical Quotations*, 1st ed. (Oxford University Press, 2004), 38.

40. Jennifer S. Lerner, Ye Li, Piercarlo Valdesolo, and Karim S. Kassam, "Emotion and Decision Making," *Annual Review of Psychology* 66, no. 1 (2015): 799–823.

41. Malcolm Gladwell, *Outliers: The Story of Success* (Little, Brown and Co., 2008).

42. Deepthi Edussuriya, Sriyani Perera, Kosala Marambe, Yomal Wijesiriwardena, and Kasun Ekanayake, "The Associates of Emotional Intelligence in Medical Students: A Systematic Review," *The Asia Pacific Scholar* 7, no. 4 (2022): 59–70, https://doi.org/10.29060/TAPS.2022-7-4/OA2714.

43. Robert M. Centor, "To Be a Great Physician, You Must Understand the Whole Story," *Medscape General Medicine* 9, no. 1 (2007): 59.

44. Dale Carnegie, *How to Win Friends and Influence People* (New York: Simon and Schuster, 2009).

45. "Good Medical Practice," General Medical Council, 2022, https://www.gmc-uk.org/professional-standards/professional-standards-for-doctors/good-medical-practice.

46. Travis Bradberry and Jean Greaves, *Emotional Intelligence 2.0*.

47. Travis Bradberry and Jean Greaves, *Emotional Intelligence 2.0*.

48. Stephen Trzeciak and Anthony Mazzarelli, *Compassionomics: The Revolutionary Scientific Evidence That Caring Makes a Difference* (Studer Group, 2019).

49. "Emotional Intelligence," Moda Image Consulting, accessed June 10, 2024, https://www.modaimageconsulting.com/individual/emotional-intelligence/.

50. "Emotional Intelligence," Digital Spark Marketing, accessed June 10, 2024, https://digitalsparkmarketing.com/emotional-intelligence/.

Chapter 6

1. R. W. Essary, "Implicit Bias Speaker: 'If You Have a Brain, You Have a Bias,'" February 23, 2020.

2. "Bias," Psychology Today, accessed June, 2024, https://www.psychologytoday.com/us/basics/bias.

3. "Bias," Psychology Today.

4. Malcolm Gladwell, *Blink: The Power of Thinking Without Thinking* (Bay Back Books, April 3, 2007).

5. Eric Wargo, "How Many Seconds to a First Impression?," Association for Psychological Science, July 1, 2006, accessed June 2024, https://www.psychologicalscience.org/observer/how-many-seconds-to-a-first-impression.

6. Jeff Bendix, "How Implicit Bias Harms Patient Care," *Medical Economics* 96, no. 23 (2019).

7. Louis A. Penner, John F. Dovidio, Richard Gonzalez, Terrance L. Albrecht, Robert Chapman, Tanina Foster, Felicity W. K. Harper, Nao Hagiwara, Lauren M. Hamel, Anthony F. Shields, Shirish Gadgeel, Michael S. Simon, Jennifer J. Griggs, and Susan Eggly, "The Effects of Oncologist Implicit Racial Bias in Racially Discordant Oncology Interactions," *Journal of Clinical Oncology* 34, no. 24 (2016): 2874–2880, doi:10.1200/JCO.2015.66.3658.

8. Chloë FitzGerald and Samia Hurst, "Implicit Bias in Healthcare Professionals: A Systematic Review," *BMC Medical Ethics* 18 (2017): 1–18, https://doi.org/10.1186/s12910-017-0179-8.

9. Alan R. Nelson, *Unequal Treatment: Confronting Racial and Ethnic Disparities in Health Care*, ed. Brian D. Smedley and Adrienne Y. Stith (National Academies Press [US], 2003), https://www.ncbi.nlm.nih.gov/books/NBK220366/.

10. Olivia Lanier, Mykel D. Green, Gilda A. Barabino, and Elizabeth Cosgriff-Hernandez, "Ten Simple Rules in Biomedical Engineering to Improve Healthcare Equity," *PLoS Computational Biology* 18, no. 10 (2022): e1010525, https://www.ncbi.nlm.nih.gov/pmc/articles/PMC9560067/.

11. "Preliminary Information," Harvard Implicit Association Test, accessed June 2024, https://implicit.harvard.edu/implicit/takeatest.html.

12. Arti Purshottam Makwana, Kristof Dhont, Esperanza García-Sancho, and Pablo Fernández-Berrocal, "Are Emotionally Intelligent People Less Prejudiced? The Importance of Emotion Management Skills for Outgroup Attitudes," *Journal of Applied Social Psychology* 51, no. 8 (2021): 779–792.

13. Vipin Jain, "The Importance of Emotional Intelligence in Effective Leadership," Culture, July 5, 2023.

14. Matthew A. Pappas, James K. Stoller, Victoria Shaker, James Houser, Anita D. Misra-Hebert, and Michael B. Rothberg, "Estimating the Costs of Physician Turnover in Hospital Medicine," *Journal of Hospital Medicine* 17, no. 10 (2022): 803–808, https://shmpublications.onlinelibrary.wiley.com/doi/10.1002/jhm.12942.

15. "2024 NSI National Health Care Retention & RN Staffing Report," NSI Nursing Solutions, Inc., accessed June 2024, https://www.nsinursingsolutions.com/Documents/Library/NSI_National_Health_Care_Retention_Report.pdf.

16. "2024 NSI National Health Care Retention & RN Staffing Report," NSI Nursing Solutions, Inc.

17. Marissa Plescia, "The Cost of Nurse Turnover By the Numbers," Financial Management, 2021.

18. Adele Lynn, *The EQ Interview: Finding Employees with High Emotional Intelligence* (AMACOM, June 9, 2008).

19. "AI-Powered Skills Assessment Tool for Recruitment," Testlify, accessed June 2024, https://testlify.com/.

20. "Exploring the Impact of Emotional Intelligence on Staff Retention and Satisfaction," ESS Global Training Solutions, accessed June 2024, https://esoftskills.com/healthcare/exploring-the-impact-of-emotional-intelligence-on-staff-retention-and-satisfaction/.

21. Britt Berrett and Paul Spiegelman, *Patients Come Second*.

Chapter 7

1. Travis Bradberry, *Self-Awareness*.

2. "Debbie Ford Quotes," BrainyQuote, accessed June 10, 2024, https://www.brainyquote.com/quotes/debbie_ford_712256.

3. Mickey Lebowitz, *Losing My Patience: Why I Quit the Medical Game*.

4. Travis Bradberry and Jean Greaves, *Emotional Intelligence 2.0* (TalentSmart, 2009), 14.

5. Robert Plutchik, "A Psychoevolutionary Theory of Emotions," *Social Science Information* 21, no. 4–5 (July 1982): 529–553. https://doi.org/10.1177/053901882021004003; "Plutchik's Wheel of Emotions: Exploring the Feelings Wheel and How to Use It (+ PDF)," Six Seconds, accessed June 10, 2024, https://www.6seconds.org/2022/03/13/plutchik-wheel-emotions/.

6. "The Emotional Intelligence Network," Six Seconds, 2024, https://www.6seconds.org/.

7. "SEI Development Report," Six Seconds, https://www.6seconds.org/tools/development-report/.

8. "Quality Quote: Those Who Do Not Learn History Are Doomed to Repeat It," Streamline Business, accessed June 10, 2024, https://streamline.business/quality-quote-those-who-do-not-learn-history-are-doomed-to-repeat-it/.

9. "SEI Development Report," Six Seconds.

Chapter 8

1. Travis Bradberry and Jean Greaves, *Emotional Intelligence 2.0*.

2. Albert Mehrabian, *Silent Messages*, 1st ed. (Belmont, CA: Wadsworth, 1971).

3. Susan Scott, *Fierce Conversations*.

4. Alan S. Cowen, Dacher Keltner, Florian Schroff, Brendan Jou, Hartwig Adam, and Gautam Prasad, "Sixteen Facial Expressions Occur in Similar Contexts Worldwide," *Nature* 589, no. 7841 (2020): 251–257.

5. "SEI Brain Profiles," Six Seconds, accessed June 10, 2024, https://www.6seconds.org/tools/profiles/.

6. "Six Seconds Emotional Intelligence Assessment (SEI)," Six Seconds, accessed June 10, 2024, https://www.6seconds.org/tools/sei/.

7. "Brain Talent Profile," Six Seconds, accessed June 10, 2024, https://www.6seconds.org/tools/brain-talent-profile/.

8. "SEI Development Report," Six Seconds.

Chapter 9

1. Dennis Aubuchon, "We Are a Product of Our Circumstances and Decisions," LinkedIn, accessed June 10, 2024, https://www.linkedin.com/pulse/we-product-our-circumstances-decisions-dennis-aubuchon/.

2. "Graham Brown," Goodreads, accessed June 10, 2024, https://www.goodreads.com/quotes/6965228-life-is-about-choices-some-we-regret-some-we-re-proud.

3. Travis Bradberry and Jean Greaves, *Emotional Intelligence 2.0* (TalentSmart, 2009), 32.

4. Daniel Kahneman, *Thinking, Fast and Slow*, 1st ed. (Farrar, Straus and Giroux, 2013).

5. Jonah Lehrer, *How We Decide*, reprint ed. (Mariner Books, 2010).

6. "SEI Development Report," Six Seconds.

7. Martin Seligman, *Learned Optimism* (Pocket Books, 1998).

8. "I've Lost Almost 300 Games," *Forbes*, accessed June 10, 2024, https://www.forbes.com/quotes/11194/.

9. Humayon Tahir, "Toxic Positivity and Mental Health: When Does Optimism Become Toxic?," September 24, 2021, https://onebehavioralhealth.com/toxic-positivity-and-mental-health-when-does-optimism-become-toxic/.

10. Ainize Sarrionandia and Moira Mikolajczak, "A Meta-Analysis of the Possible Behavioural and Biological Variables Linking Trait Emotional Intelligence to Health," *Health Psychology Review* 14, no. 2 (2020): 220–244.

Chapter 10

1. Waqar Husain, Samia Wasif, and Insha Fatima, "Profanity as a Self-Defense Mechanism and an Outlet for Emotional Catharsis in Stress, Anxiety, and Depression," *Depression Research and Treatment* 2023, no.1 (2023): 8821517.

2. "Name It to Tame It: Label Your Emotions to Overcome Negative Thoughts," Mindful.com, accessed June 10, 2024, https://mindfulness.com/mindful-living/name-it-to-tame-it.

3. Daniel Siegel and Tina Bryson, *The Whole-Brain Child*.

4. Marc A. Russo, Danielle M. Santarelli, and Dean O'Rourke, "The Physiological Effects of Slow Breathing in the Healthy Human," *Breathe* 13, no. 4 (2017): 298–309, doi:10.1183/20734735.009817.

5. The term "emotional escalator" does not appear to be widely attributed to a specific individual or original source in the available literature. It seems to be a concept discussed more generally in the context of emotional intelligence and emotional regulation rather than being coined by a particular person.

Chapter 11

1. Michael Lewis, *The Undoing Project: A Friendship That Changed Our Minds* (W. W. Norton & Company, 2016).

2. "5 Benefits of Healthy Relationships: Why Healthy Relationships Are So Important," HealthBeat, September 2021, https://www.nm.org/healthbeat/ healthy-tips/5-benefits-of-healthy-relationships.

3. Robert Waldinger and Marc Schulz, "What the Longest Study on Human Happiness Found Is the Key to a Good Life," *The Atlantic*, January 19, 2023.

4. "8 Reasons Why It's Important to Build Workplace Relationships," Indeed, updated February 28, 2023, https://www.indeed.com/career-advice/ career-development/importance-of-building-relationships.

5. Tania Farran, "Connecting with Your Students," Udemy, November 2022, https://www.udemy.com/course/ connecting-motivating-and-building-relationships/.

6. Ali Grovue and Mike Watson, "The Five C's of Trust," Chief Executive, April 27, 2022, https://chiefexecutive.net/the-five-cs-of-trust/.

7. Paul Gewirtz, "On 'I Know It When I See It,'" *Yale LJ* 105 (1995): 1023, https://openyls.law.yale.edu/bitstream/handle/20.500.13051/8935/38_105 YaleLJ1023_January1996_.pdf?sequence=2&isAllowed=y.

8. Susan Scott, *Fierce Conversations*.

9. Vadim Kotelnikov, "Face-to-Face Communication," https://www.1000 ventures.com/business_guide/crosscuttings/communication_f2f.html.

10. Albert Mehrabian, *Silent Messages*.

11. "Illuminate: Feeling Stuck? Try This 3-Step Technique," Six Seconds, accessed June 10, 2024, https://www.6seconds.org/2019/10/07/illuminate-feeling-stuck-try-this-3-step-technique/.

12. Dale Carnegie, *How to Win Friends and Influence People*.

13. Dale Carnegie, *How to Win Friends and Influence People*.

14. Dale Carnegie, *How to Win Friends and Influence People*.

15. Michael J. Lee, "On Patient Safety: Do You Say 'I'm Sorry' to Patients?," *Clinical Orthopaedics and Related Research* 474, no. 11 (2016): 2359–2361.

16. "Albert Einstein," Goodreads, https://www.goodreads.com/quotes/987-there-are-only-two-ways-to-live-your-life-one.

17. Travis Bradberry and Jean Greaves, *Emotional Intelligence 2.0* (TalentSmart, 2009), 179.

18. Kathy Petras and Ross Petras, "If You Use These 13 Phrases Every Day, You Have Higher Emotional Intelligence 'Than Most People': Psychology Experts," *CNBC*, April 1, 2023, https://www.cnbc.com/2023/04/01/if-you-use-these-phrases-every-day-you-have-high-emotional-intelligence-say-psychology-experts.html.

19. "35 Quotes About Communication for Inspiring Team Collaboration," Vibe, May 5, 2022, https://vibe.us/blog/35-quotes-about-communication/?srsltid=AfmBOorVMWddDB0HsR9hiLw14uUNcp8La5jJODhtn-tQgyWKfs2Z6Hk0.

20. A. Rauf Ganatra, "Touching You," Pinterest, https://www.pinterest.com/pin/308074430732734219/.

21. Purpose Cravings, "Cravings Quotes," Pinterest, https://www.pinterest.com/pin/716002040748545450/.

22. James Redfield, *The Celestine Prophecy* (Sartori Publishing, 1993).

23. John W. Ayers, Adam Poliak, Mark Dredze, Eric C. Leas, Zechariah Zhu, Jessica B. Kelley, Dennis J. Faix, Aaron M. Goodman, Christopher A. Longhurst, Michael Hogarth, and Davey M. Smith, "Comparing Physician and Artificial Intelligence Chatbot Responses to Patient Questions Posted to a Public Social Media Forum," *JAMA Internal Medicine* 183, no. 6 (2023): 589–596, doi:10.1001/jamainternmed.2023.1838.

24. David Brooks, *How to Know a Person: The Art of Seeing Others Deeply and Being Deeply Seen* (Random House, 2023).

Chapter 12

1. "Self-Direct," Merriam-Webster, https://www.merriam-webster.com/dictionary/self-direct.

2. Oprah Winfrey, "What Oprah Knows for Sure About Finding Your Calling," Oprah.com, https://www.oprah.com/spirit/oprah-on-finding-your-calling-what-i-know-for-sure.

3. Susan Scott, *Fierce Conversations*.

4. Stephen Trzeciak and Anthony Mazzarelli, *Wonder Drug: 7 Scientifically Proven Ways That Serving Others Is the Best Medicine for Yourself* (St. Martin's Essentials, June 21, 2022).

5. "SEI Development Report," Six Seconds.

6. "SEI Development Report," Six Seconds.

7. "Angie's Motivation: 'If Today Was the Last Day of My Life,'" The Morning Hustle, posted on Facebook, February 24, 2021, https://www.facebook.com/MorningHustleShow/videos/angies-motivation-if-today-was-the-last-day-of-my-life-steve-jobs/469557614080811/.

8. "Go to Bed Smarter Than When You Woke Up," Mickmel, November 2, 2022, https://www.mickmel.com/go-to-bed-smarter-than-when-you-woke-up/.

9. Kerry Patterson, Joseph Grenny, Ron McMillan, and Al Switzler, *Crucial Conversations: Tools for Talking When Stakes Are High*, 2nd ed. (McGraw Hill, 2011).

10. "110 Leadership Quotes: Daily Doses of Inspiration to Unlock Greatness," ITD World, accessed June 5, 2024, https://itdworld.com/blog/leadership/leadership-quotes/.

11. "Leo Buscaglia Quotes," BrainyQuote, accessed June 5, 2024, https://www.brainyquote.com/quotes/leo_buscaglia_106299.

12. Dano Moreno, "Empathy Is Medicine."

13. Stephen Trzeciak and Anthony Mazzarelli, *Compassionomics*.

14. J. D. Meier, "Great Emotional Intelligence Quotes," Sources of Insight, https://sourcesofinsight.com/emotional-intelligence-quotes/.

15. Bashier Alqarni, "Inside Out: Sadness Comforts Bing Bong," video uploaded to YouTube, accessed June 5, 2024, https://www.youtube.com/watch?v=QT6FdhKriB8.

16. Diana Simon Psihoterapeut, "Brené Brown on Empathy vs. Sympathy," video uploaded to YouTube, accessed June 5, 2024, https://www.youtube.com/watch?v=KZBTYViDPlQ.

17. "Compassion Fatigue," Merriam-Webster Online Dictionary, accessed March 5, 2025, https://www.merriam-webster.com/dictionary/compassion%20fatigue.

18. R. W. Essary, "Implicit Bias Speaker."

19. "Empathy: The Human Connection to Patient Care," video uploaded to YouTube, accessed June 5, 2024, https://www.youtube.com/watch?v=cDDWvj_q-o8.

20. Vincent J. Felitti, Robert F. Anda, Dale Nordenberg, David F. Williamson, Alison M. Spitz, Valerie Edwards, and James S. Marks, "Relationship of Childhood Abuse and Household Dysfunction to Many of the Leading Causes of Death in Adults: The Adverse Childhood Experiences (ACE) Study," *American Journal of Preventive Medicine* 14, no. 4 (1998): 245–258, doi:10.1016/S0749-3797(98)00017-8.

21. "Dr Brené Brown: Empathy vs Sympathy," Twenty One Toys, accessed June 5, 2024, https://twentyonetoys.com/blogs/teaching-empathy/brene-brown-empathy-vs-sympathy.

22. "Goals of Care Conversations Training for Physicians, Advance Practice Nurses, & Physician Assistants," U.S. Department of Veterans Affairs, updated January 3, 2019, accessed March 26, 2025, https://www.ethics.va.gov/goalsofcaretraining/practitioner.asp.

23. Robert Glazer, "Sympathy & Empathy Are Not The Same—Here's Why It Matters For Leaders," LinkedIn, accessed June 5, 2024, https://www.linkedin.com/pulse/sympathy-empathy-same-heres-why-matters-leaders-robert-glazer/.

24. Rebecca O'Donnell, *Freak: The True Story of an Insecurity Addict* (Authorhouse, 2011).

25. Donna Marino, "Are you Suffering from High Achievers Syndrome?," LinkedIn, accessed June 5, 2024, https://www.linkedin.com/pulse/you-suffering-from-high-achievers-syndrome-marino-psyd-cipp-ppc/.

26. Helen Reiss and Liz Neporent, *The Empathy Effect: Seven Neuroscience-Based Keys for Transforming the Way We Live, Love, Work, and Connect Across Differences* (Sounds True, November 27, 2018).

Conclusion

1. "When did Albert Einstein say the quote: 'The measure of intelligence is the ability to change'?," accessed April 9, 2025, Brainly, https://brainly.com/question/36839548.

2. Daniel Goleman, *Emotional Intelligence.*

Appendix

1. Joshua Freedman, "Coaching Down the Escalator: 3 Emotional Intelligence Tips for Coaches to Reduce Volatility & De-escalate Conflict in a Polarized World," Six Seconds, accessed April 9, 2025, https://www.6seconds.org/2024/03/06/coaching-reduce-conflict.

About the Author

Mickey Lebowitz, originally from Brooklyn, New York, is a graduate of SUNY-Oswego (magna cum laude and student athlete of the year) and Upstate Medical University (AOA, cum laude) and a board-certified endocrinologist/diabetologist (Fellow, American College of Endocrinology). He has worked in a physician-owned practice, as an employed physician, in the VA system, and currently as an endocrine hospitalist. He spent seven years as a hospital-based senior medical quality director and is currently a chief medical officer at a health-care transportation company. He's an educator, serving as the medical director of a physician assistant program in upstate New York, and an author, whose first book, *Losing My Patience*, was published in 2009. Through Six Seconds, he is a certified assessor, practitioner, facilitator, and coach in emotional intelligence (EQ), coaching clinicians, nurses, and health-care students on leadership, professionalism, and interpersonal relationships.

He has given countless presentations and workshops on EQ locally and nationally and is in the process of publishing his research on the impact of EQ on his PA programs' students. He has been on the list of Best Doctors in America, is an honoree of the Juvenile Diabetes Research Foundation (Breakthrough T1D), and has received awards for preceptor and resident teaching, community service for educating health-care professionals on wellness and burnout, dedication and loyalty to the medical profession, excellence in health-care education, as well as the NYSSPA Physician Advocate of the Year award.

Dr. Mickey is most proud of being married to his wonderful wife since 1982, having two fabulous children with awesome spouses and three precious granddaughters, whom he is in love with, head over heels. For fun he likes to exercise by walking, biking, hiking, swimming, and kayaking. He loves traveling, writing songs, rapping (yes, rapping!), and volunteers heavily in his faith and secular community, and he is a FANatic rooting for his favorite teams.